VISUAL ILLUSIONS

SPYROS HOREMIS
KOICHI SATO

3-D GLASSES INSIDE!

DOVER PUBLICATIONS, INC.
MINEOLA, NEW YORK

GREEN
EDITION ®

Bibliographical Note

3-D Coloring Book: Visual Illusions, first published by Dover Publications, Inc., in 2011 contains all the plates from the following previously published Dover books: *Visual Illusions Coloring Book* (1973) by Spyros Horemis and *Optical Illusions Coloring Book* (1994) by Koichi Sato.

International Standard Book Number
ISBN-13: 978-0-486-48926-1
ISBN-10: 0-486-48926-4

Manufactured in the United States by Courier Corporation
48926403
www.doverpublications.com

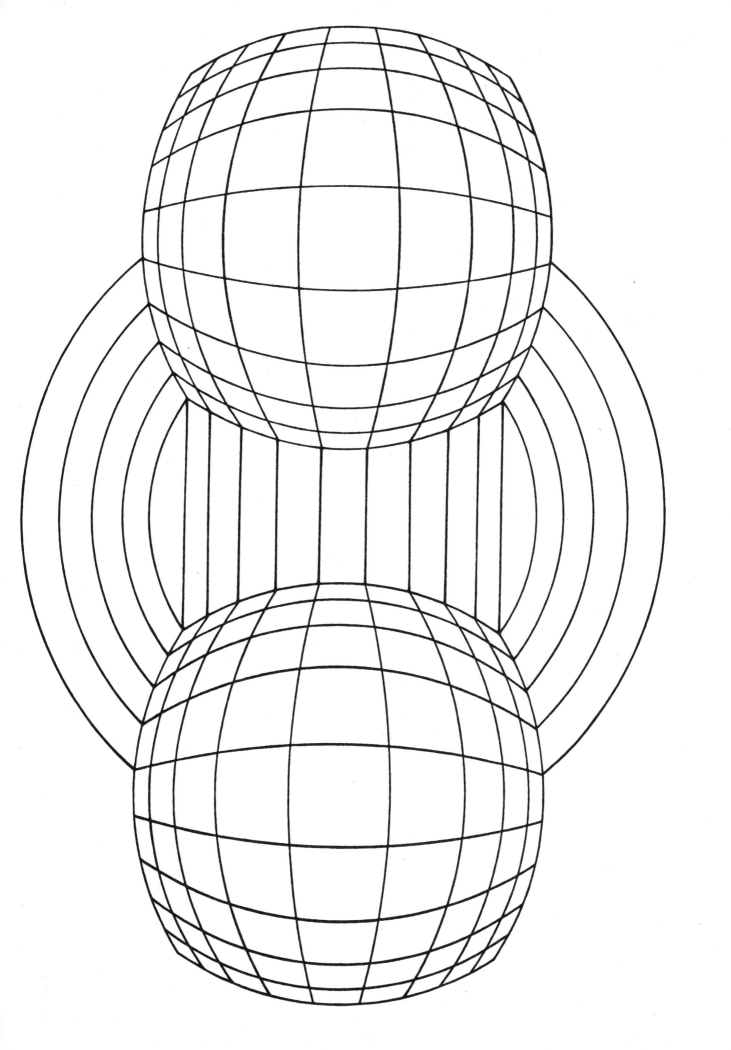

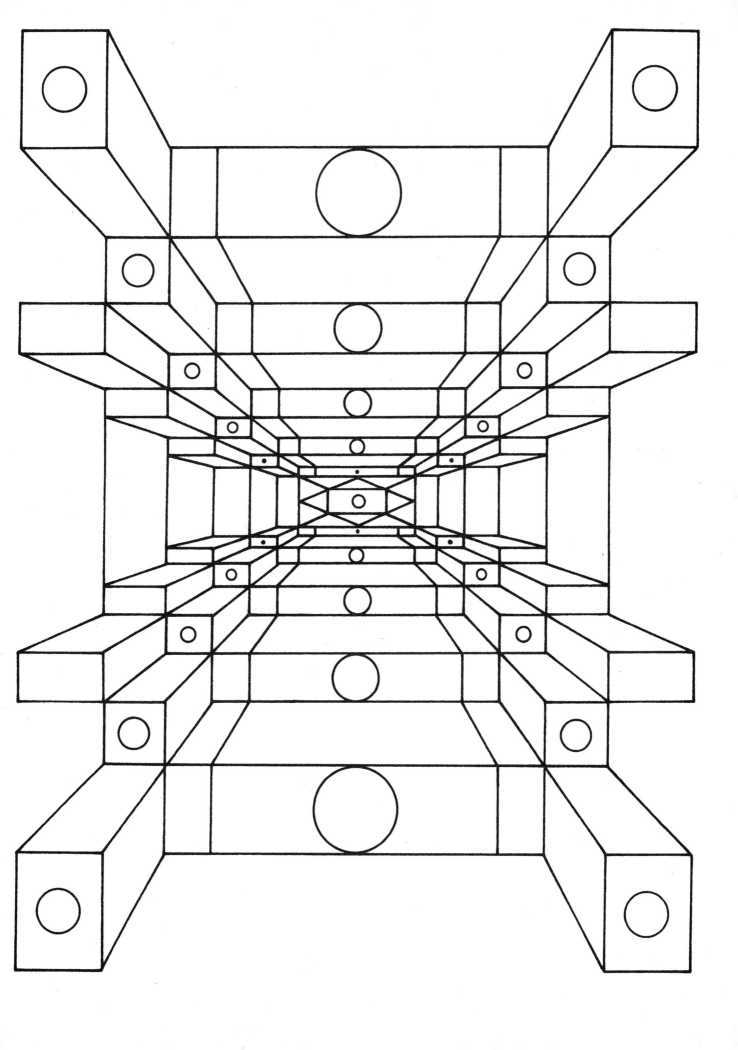

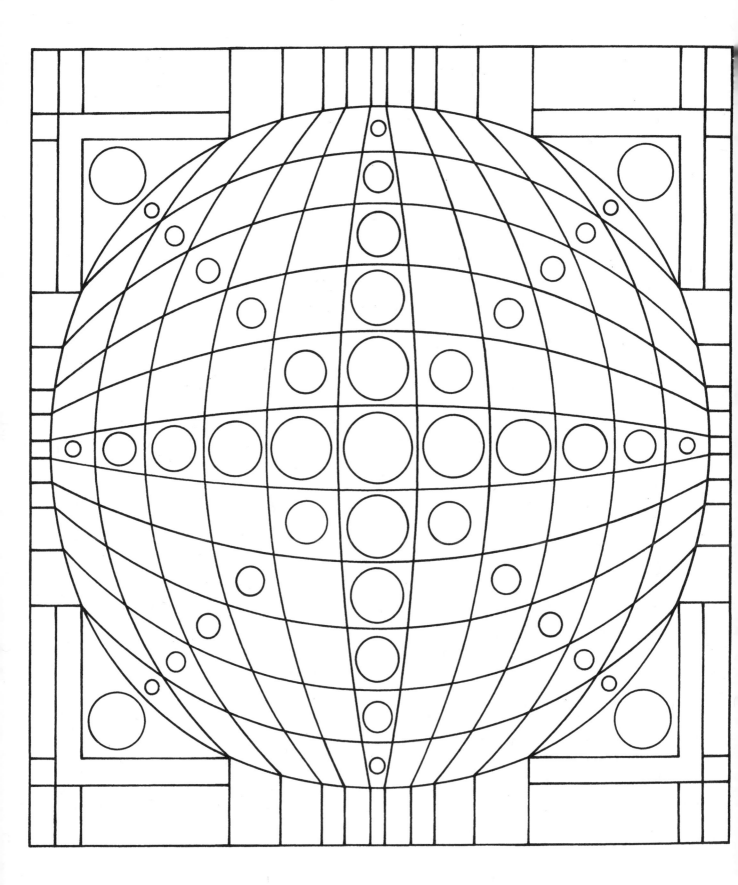

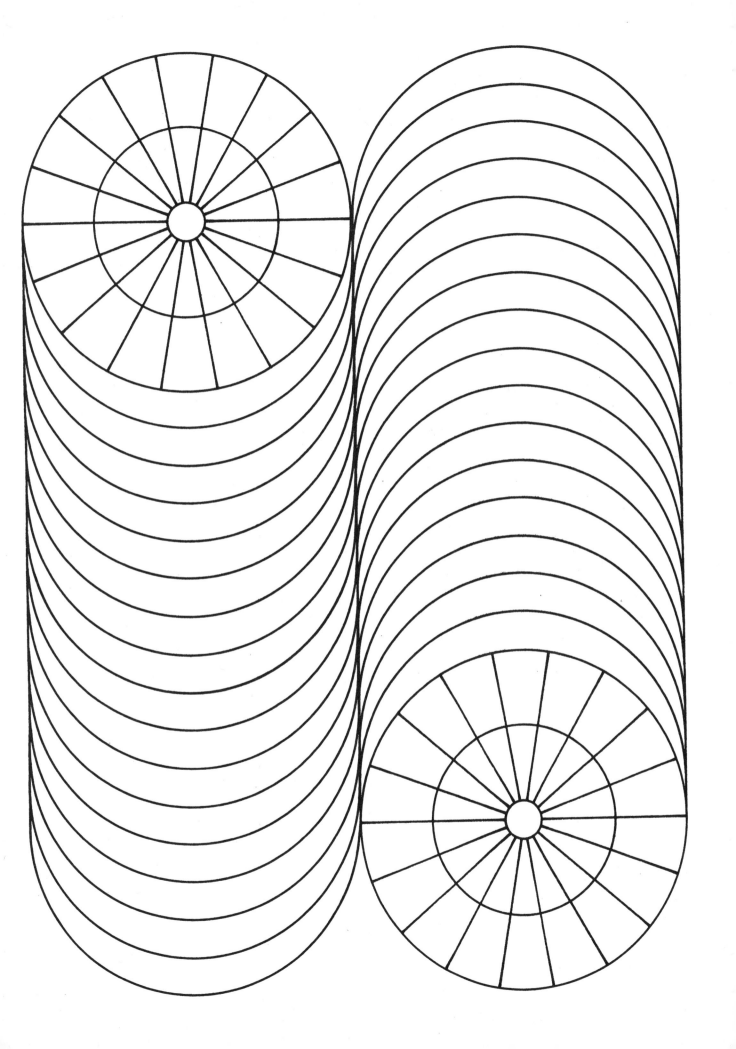

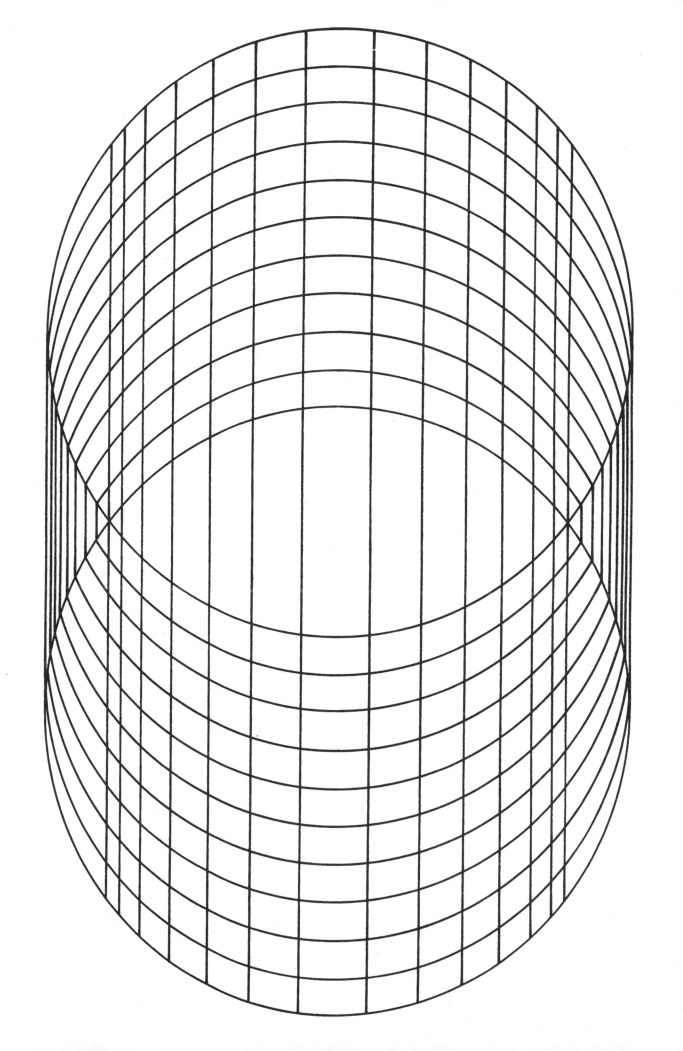

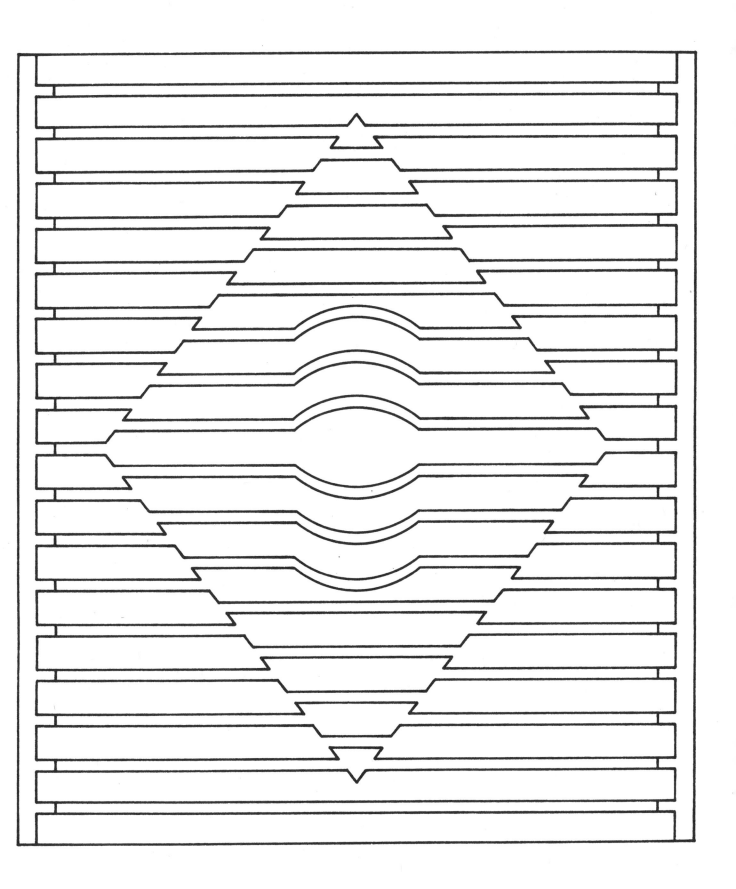

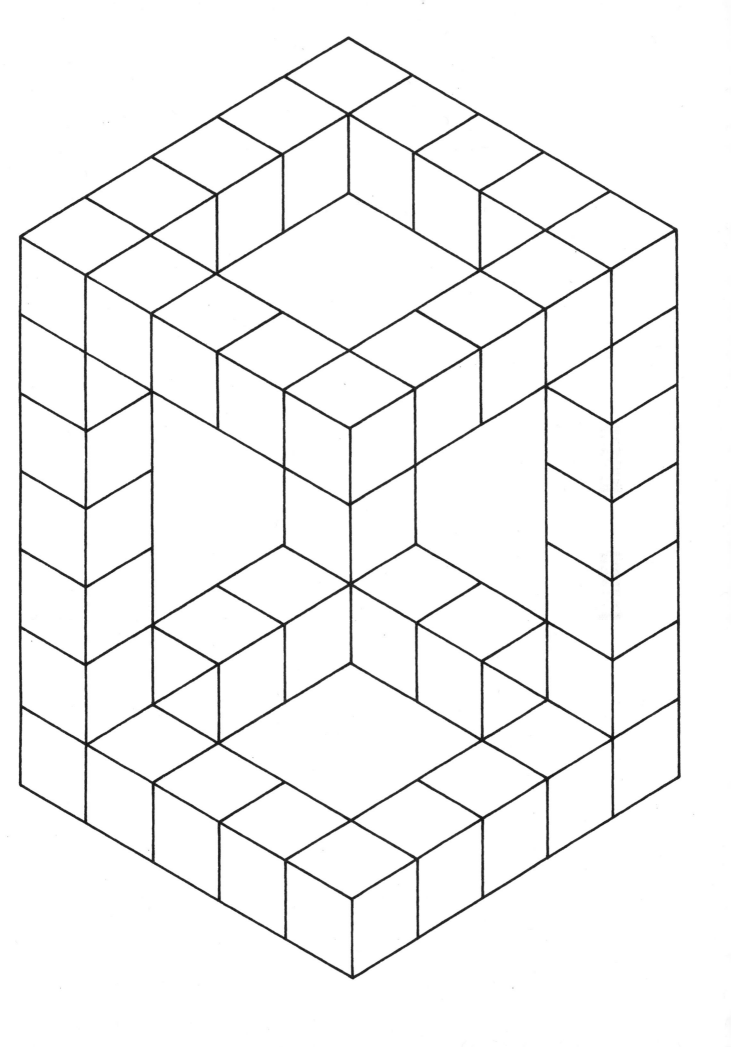

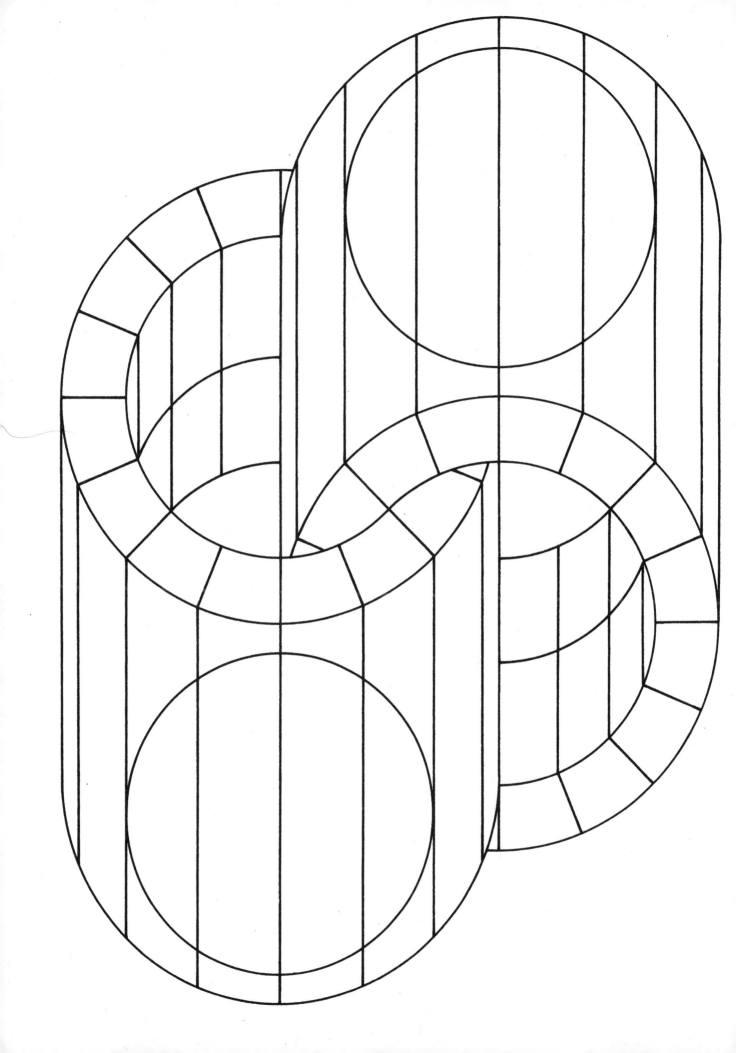

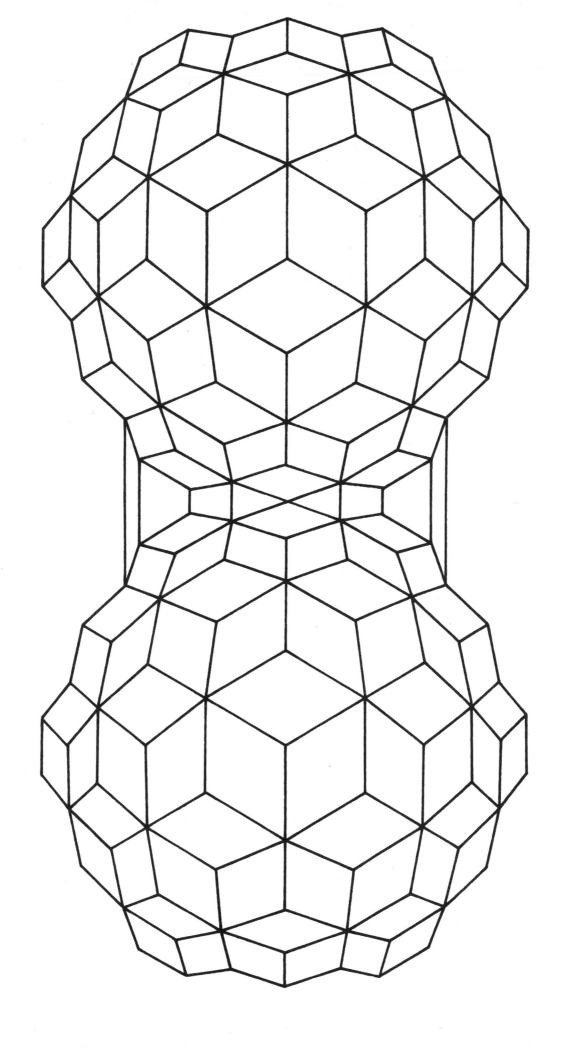

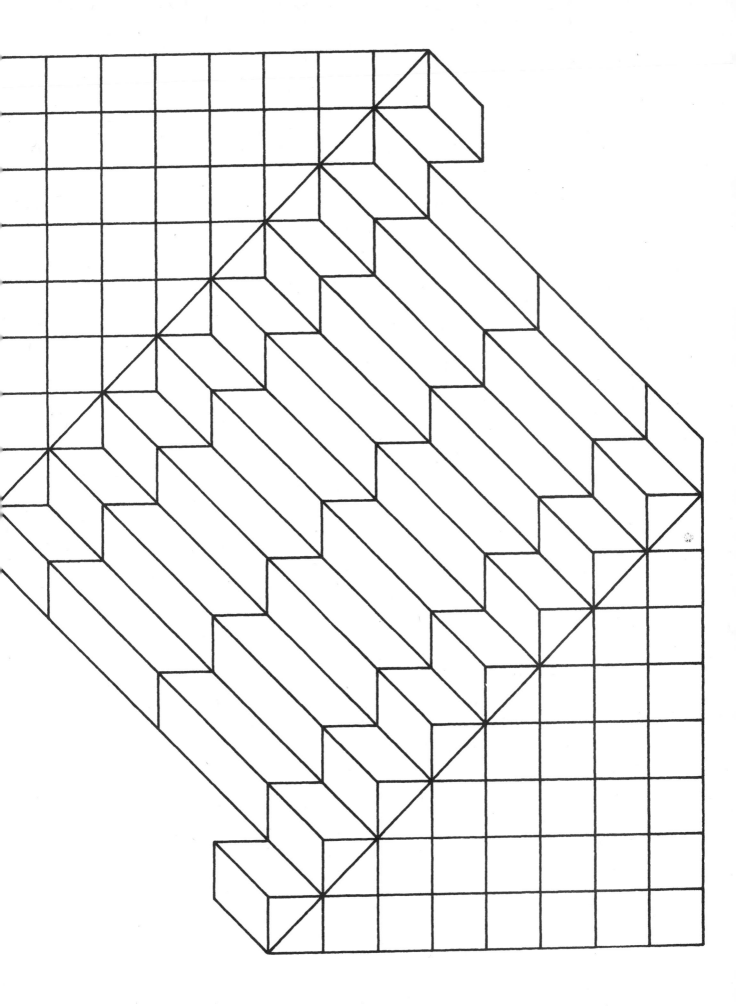

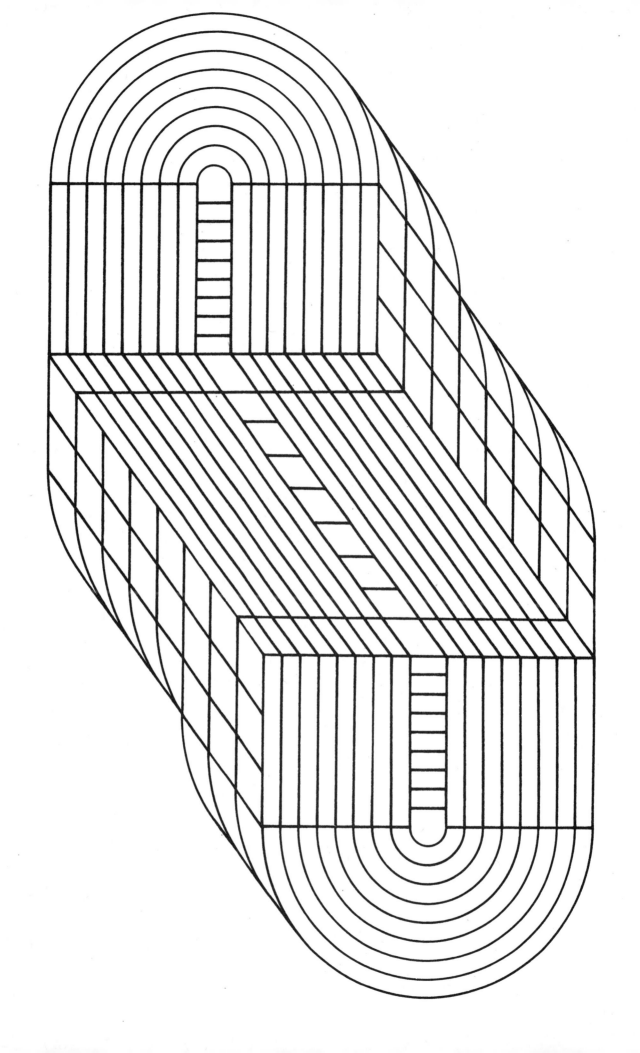

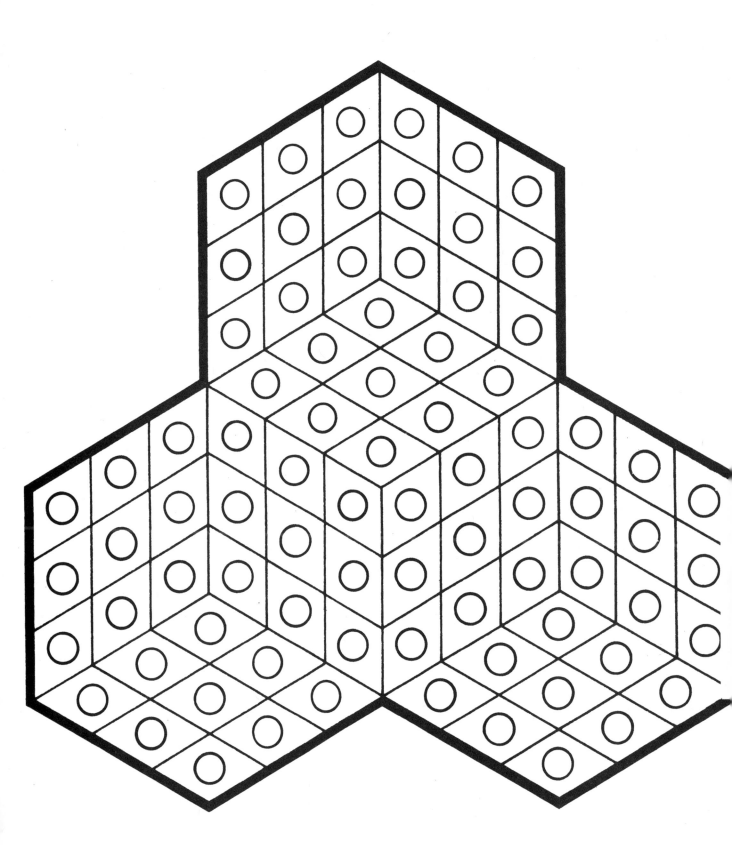

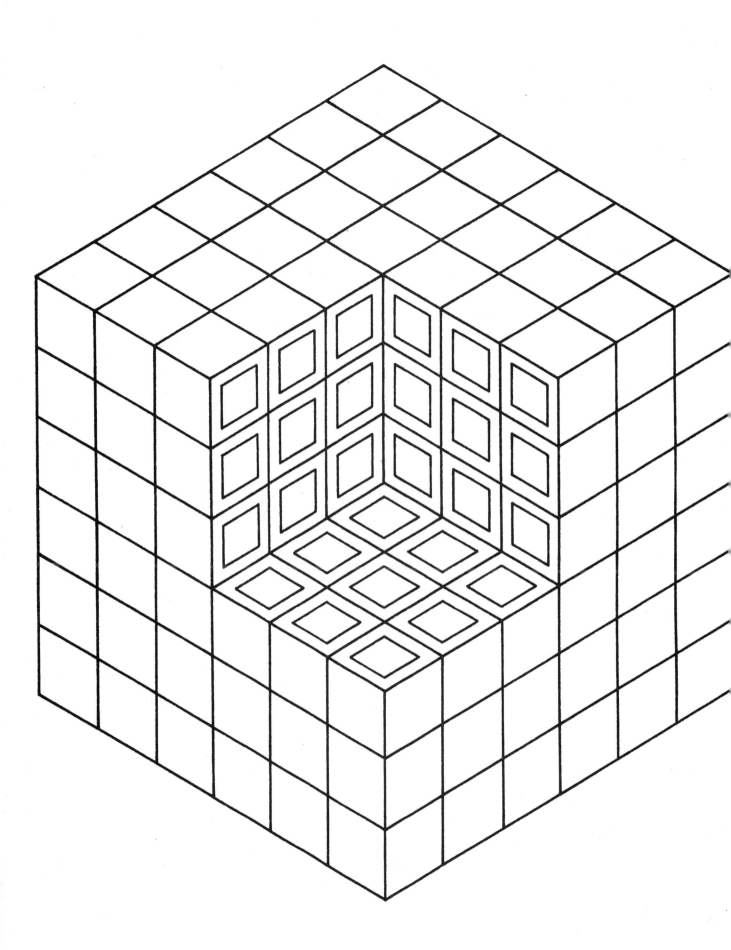

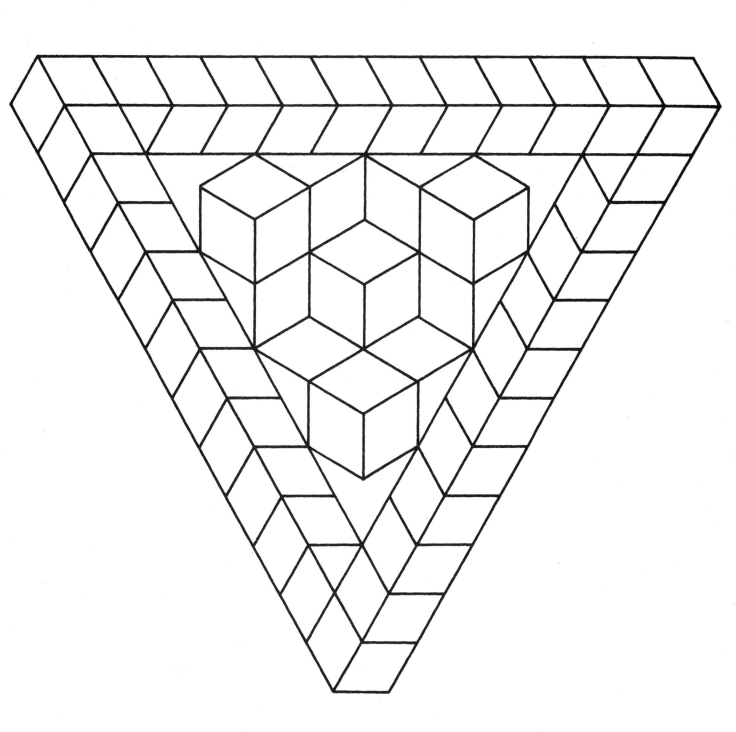

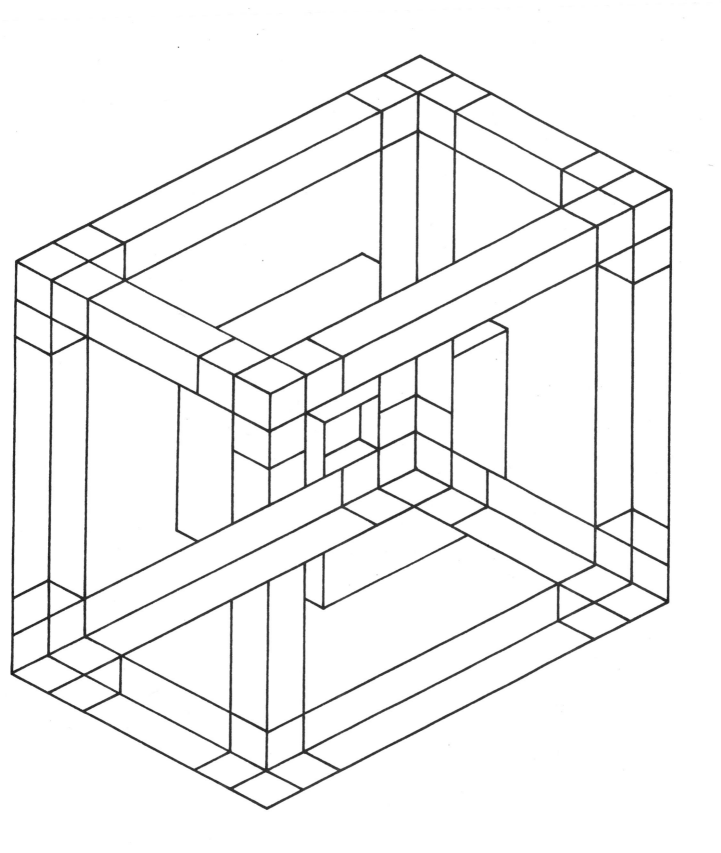

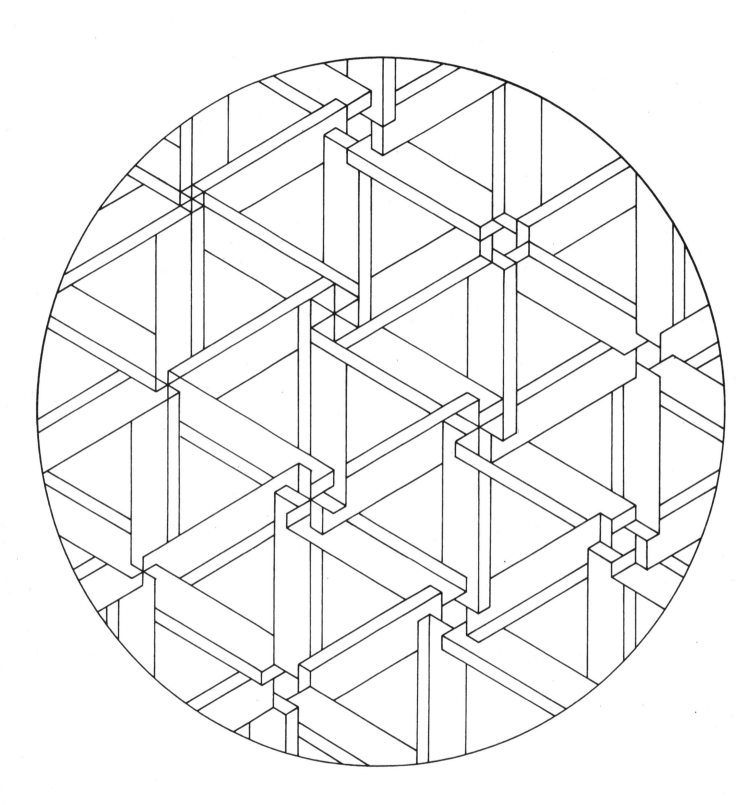

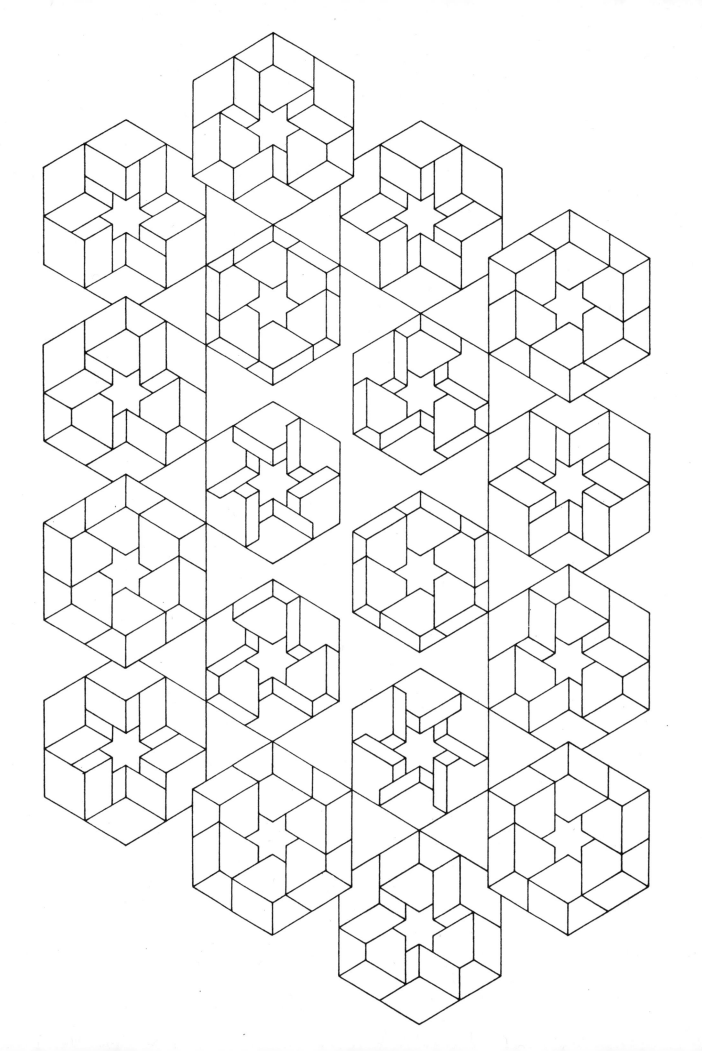

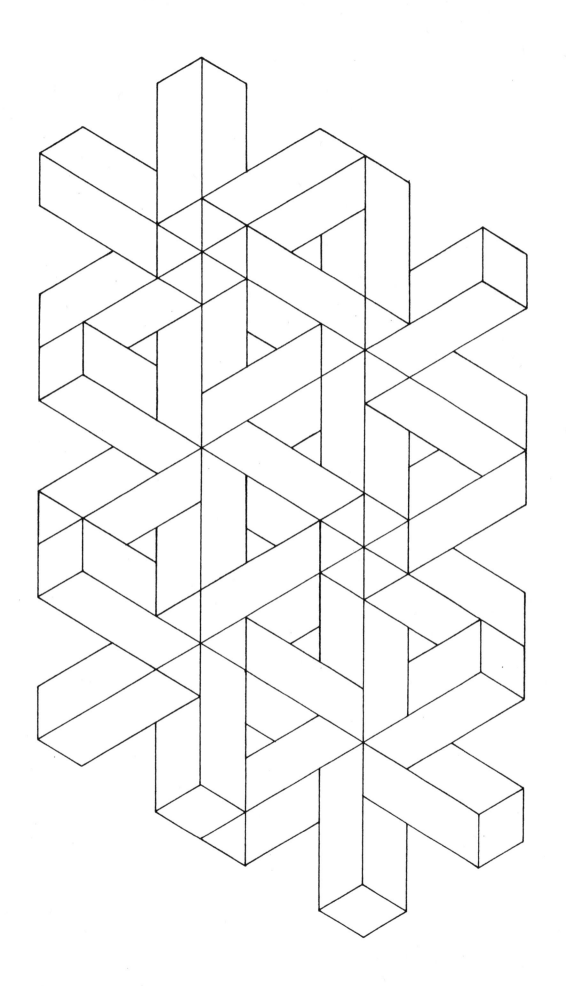

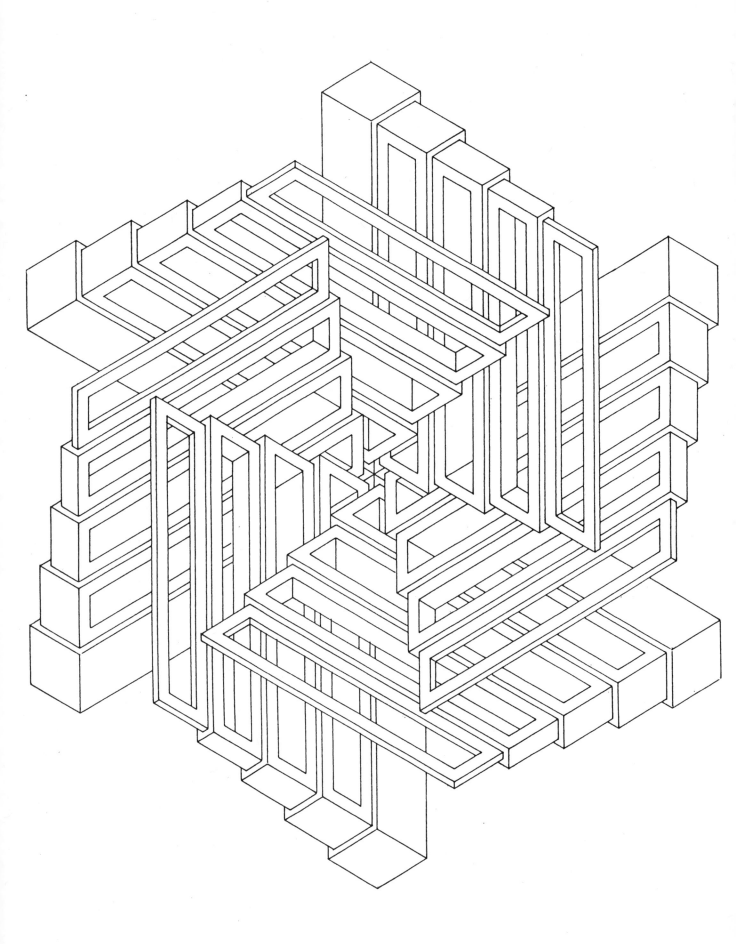

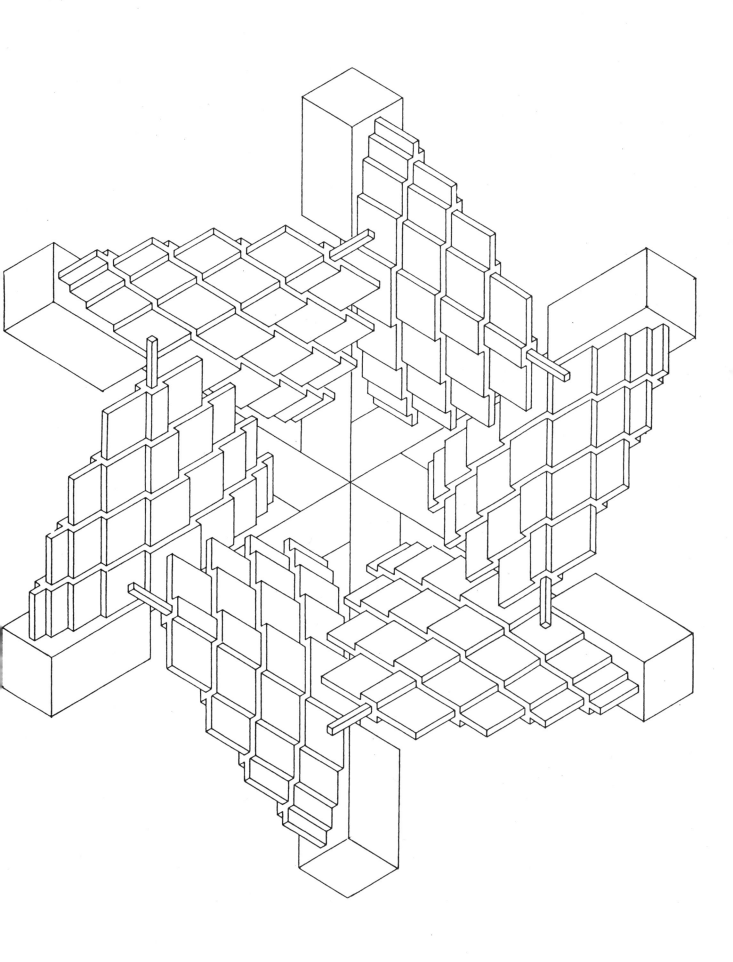

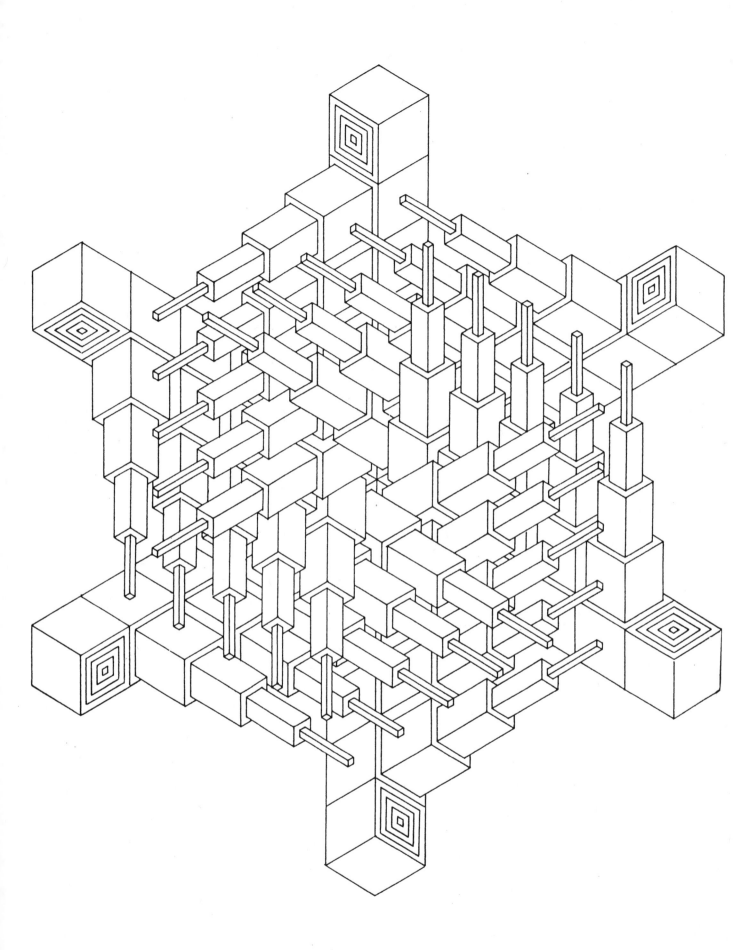

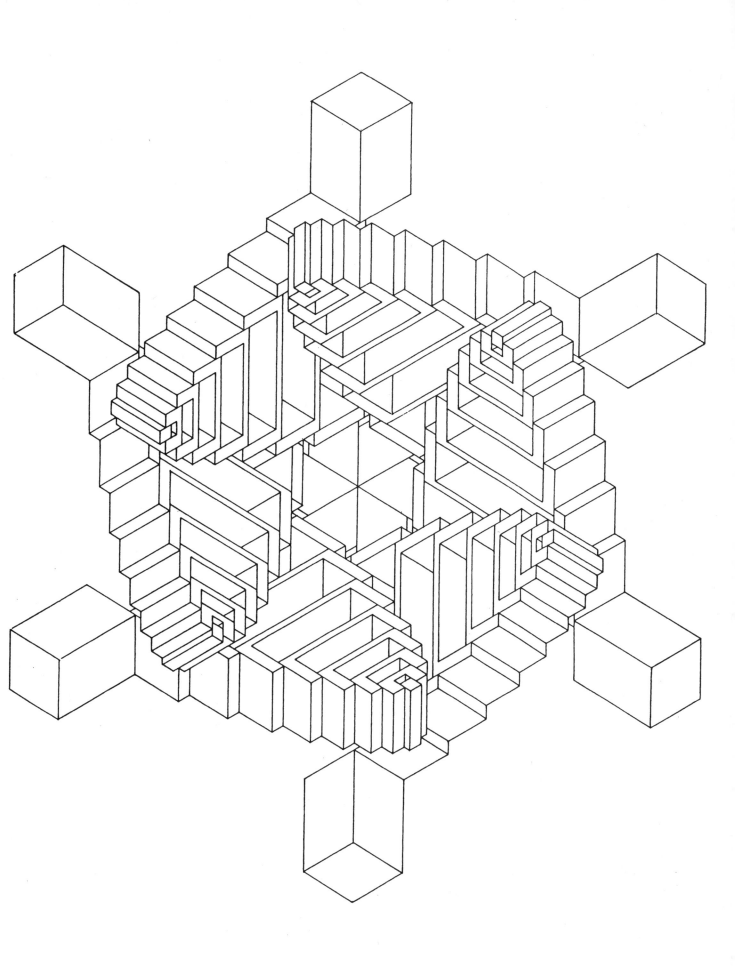

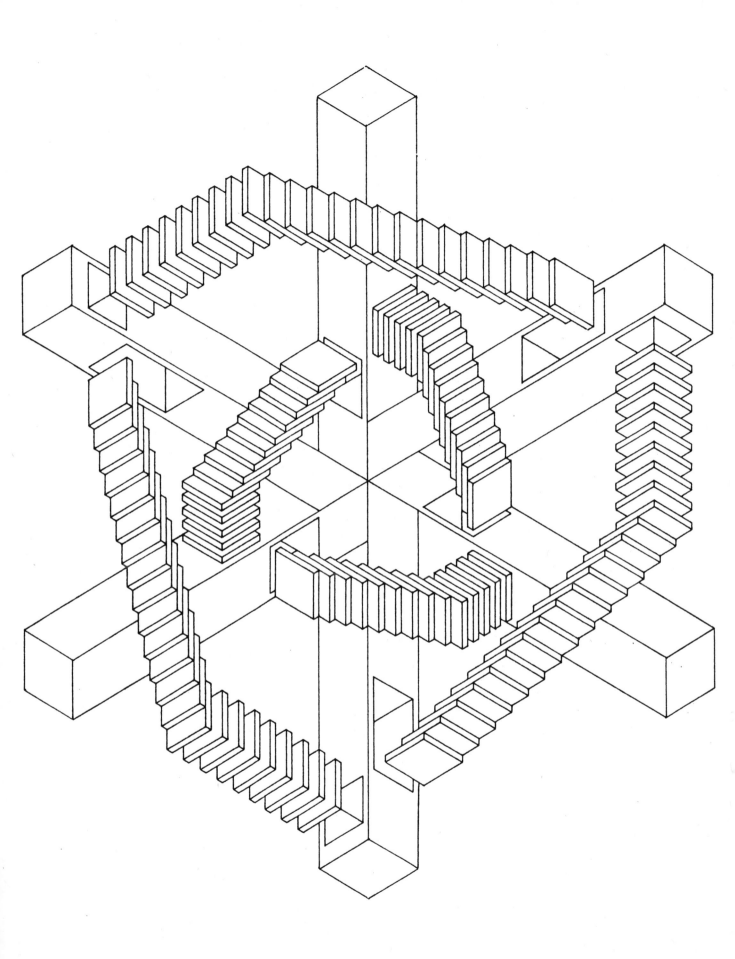

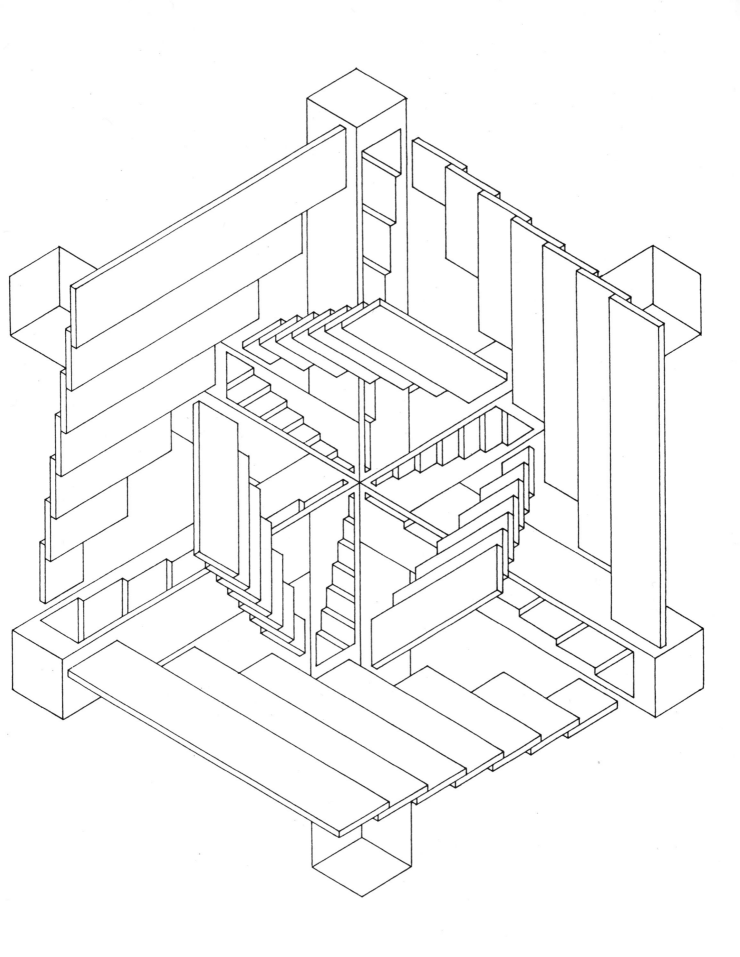

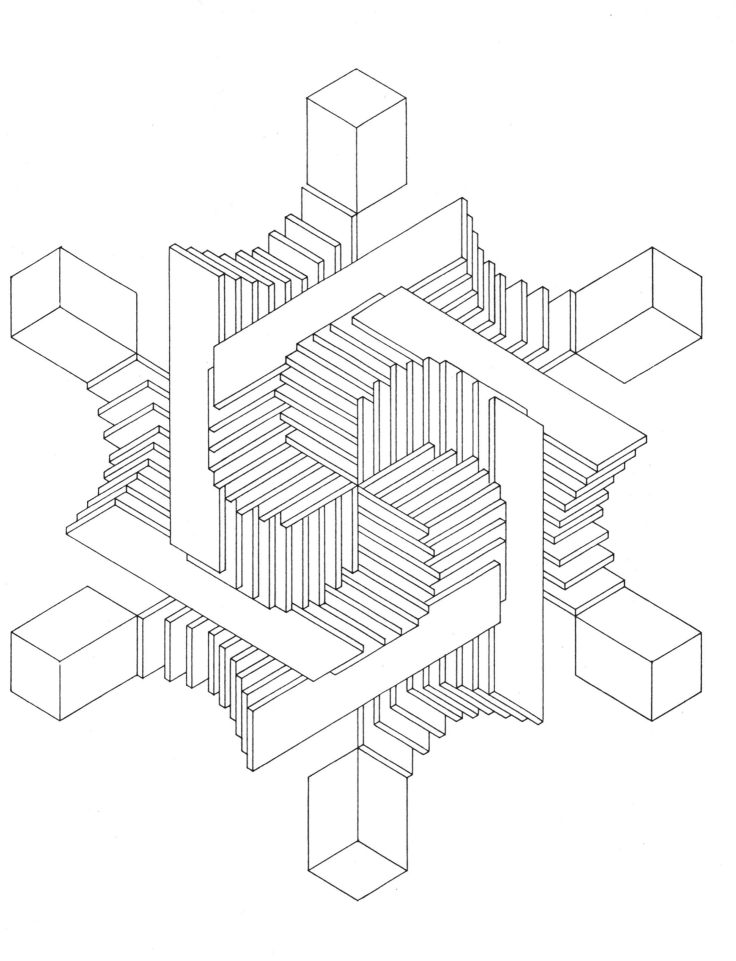

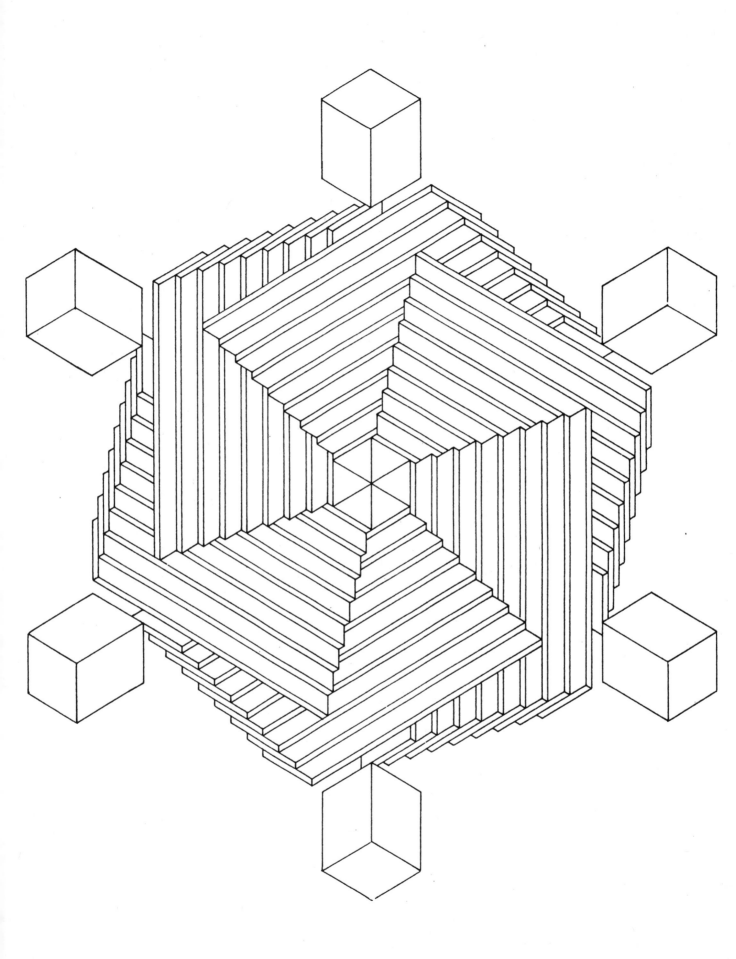

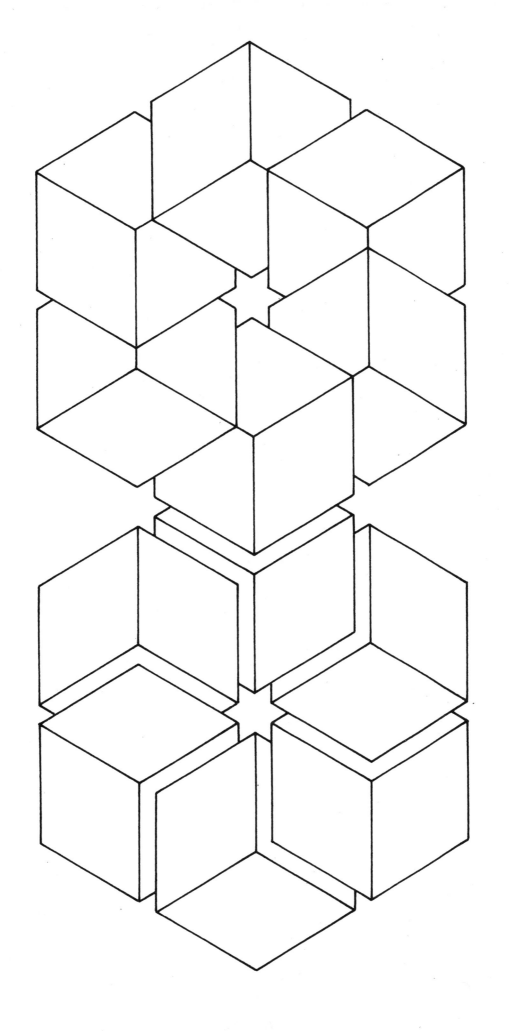

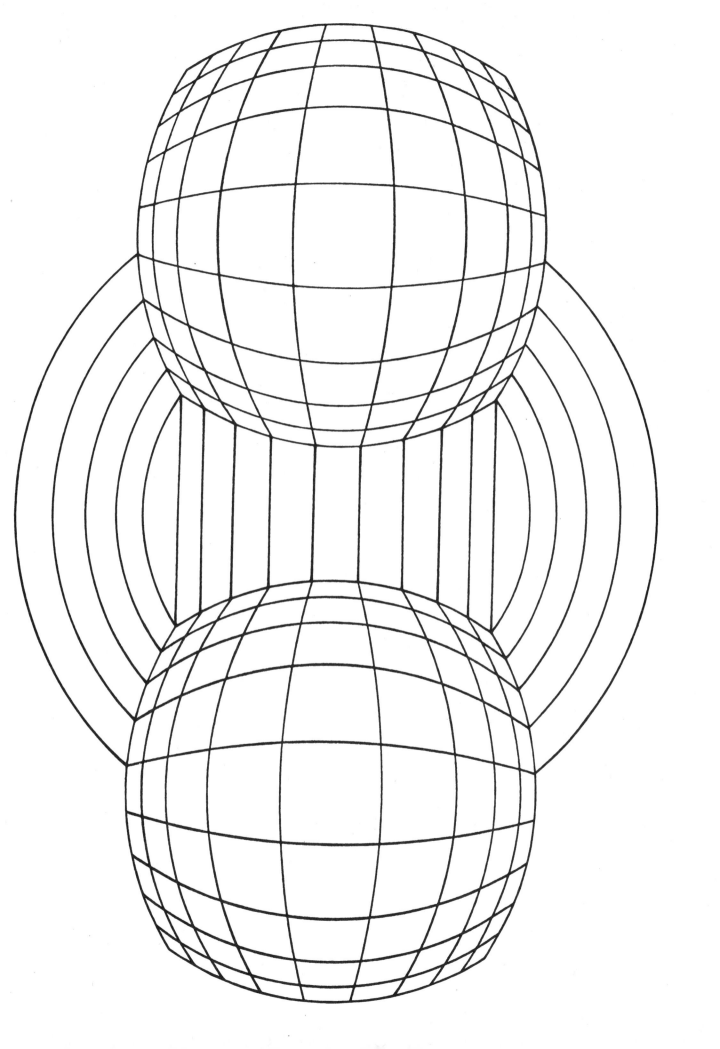

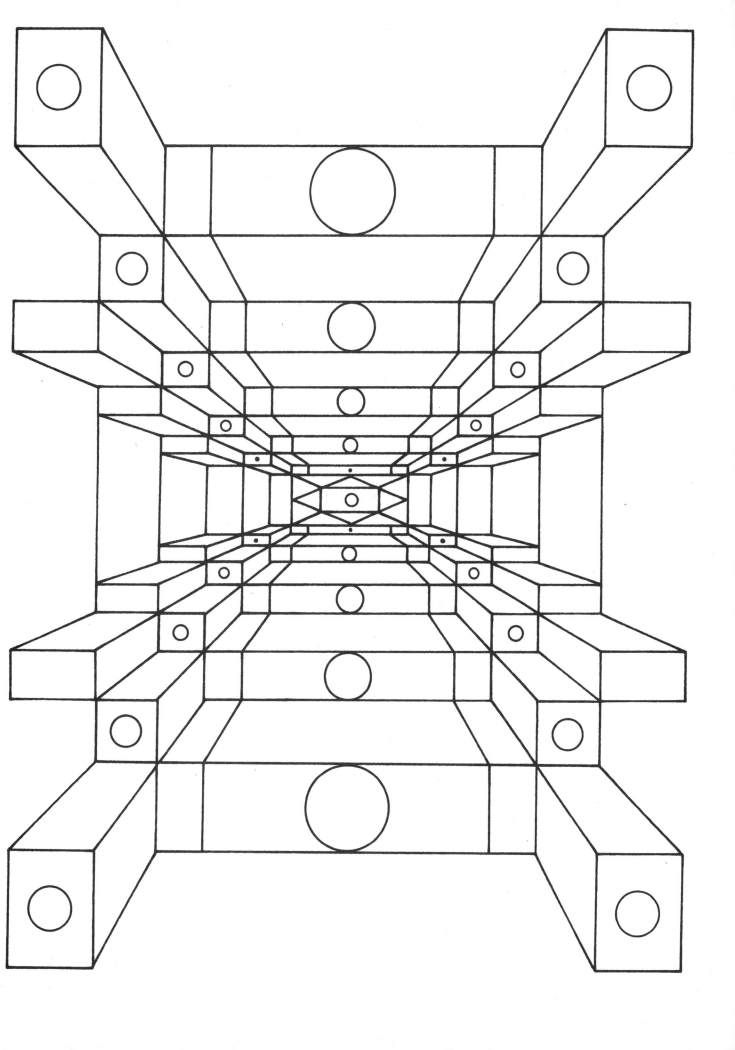

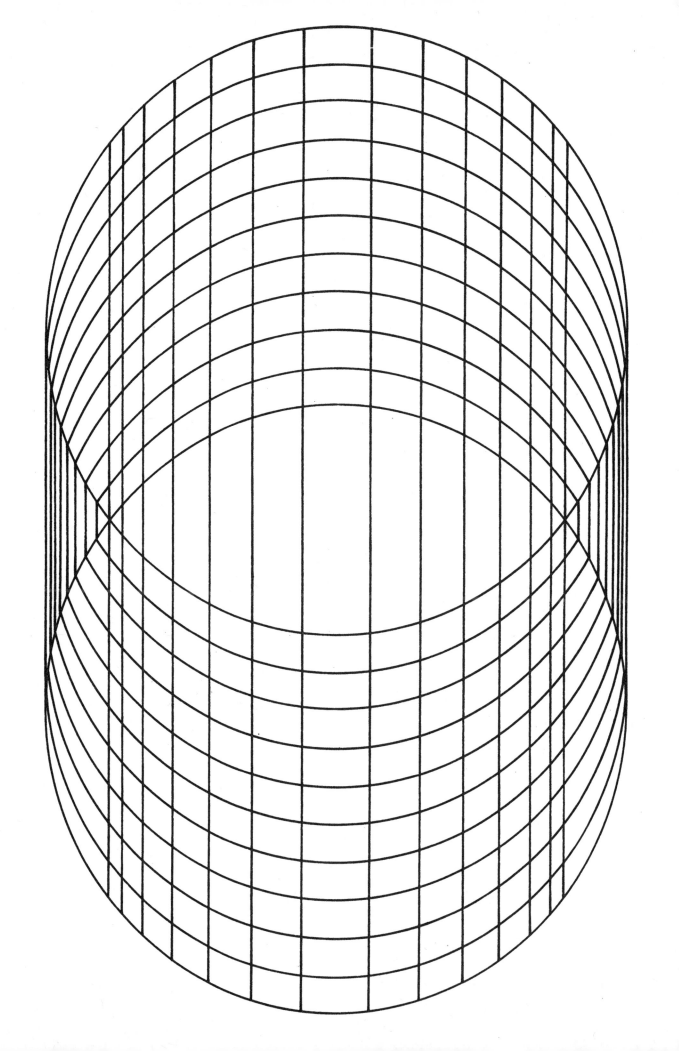

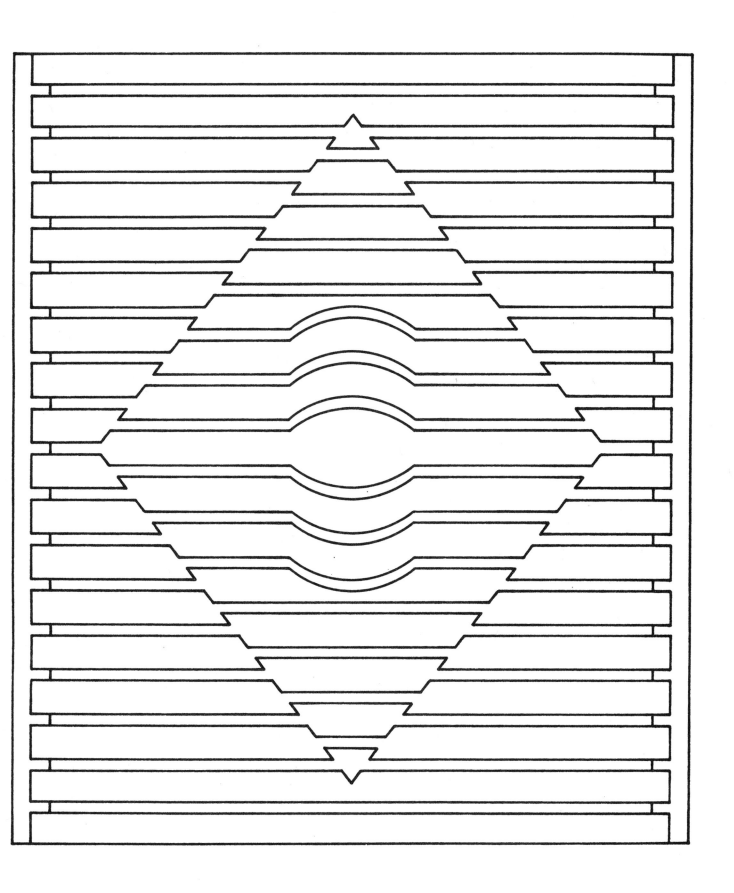

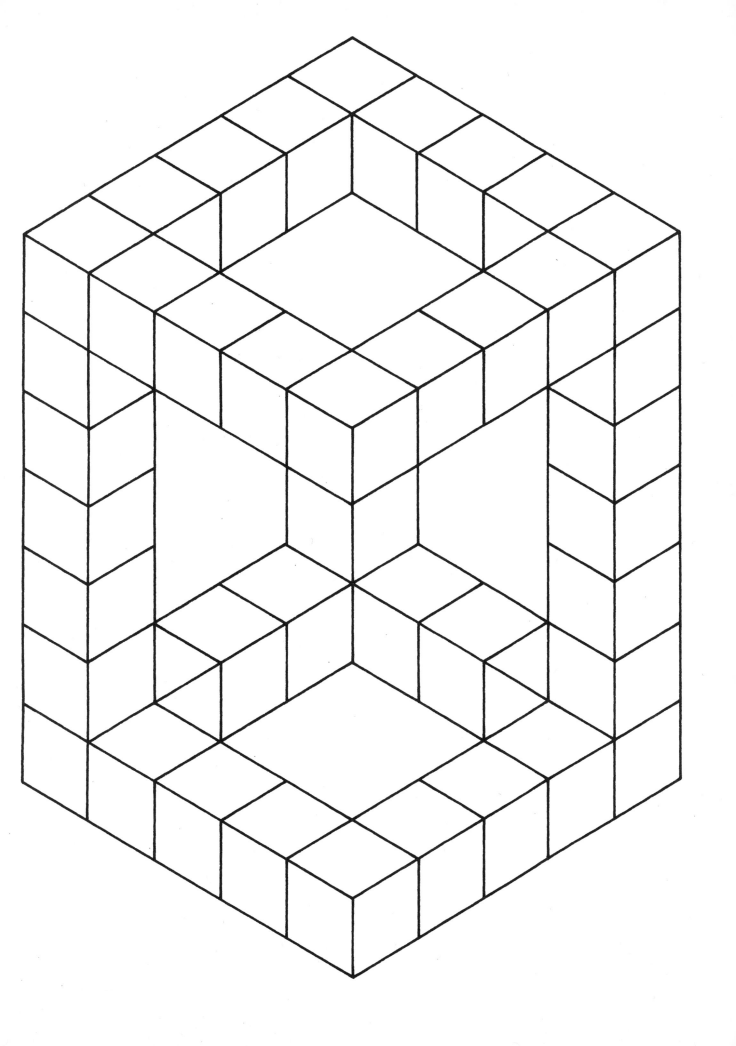

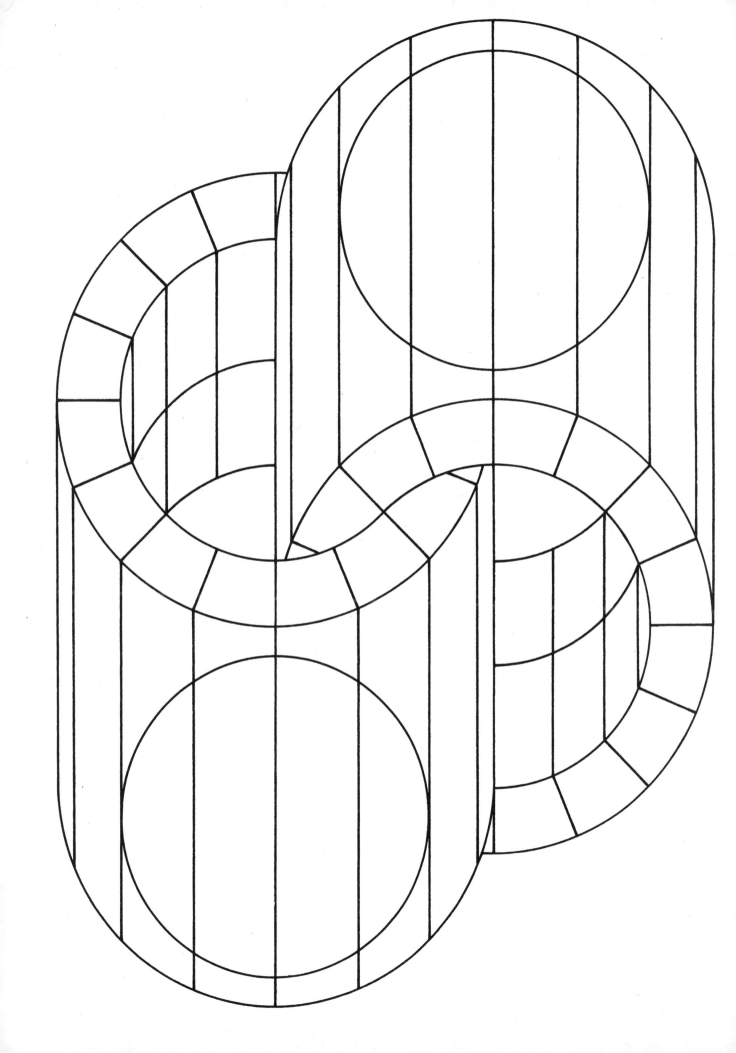

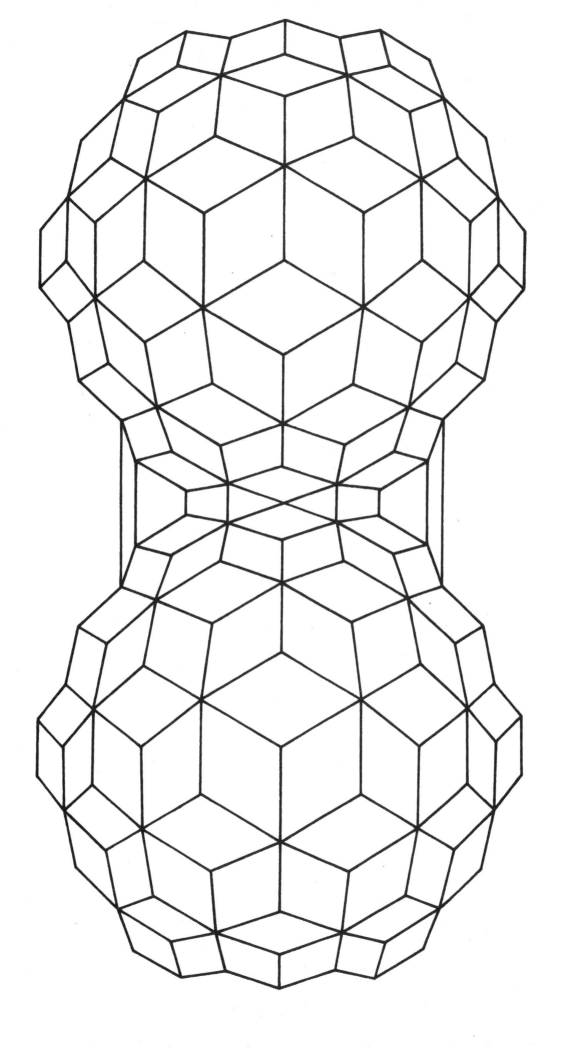

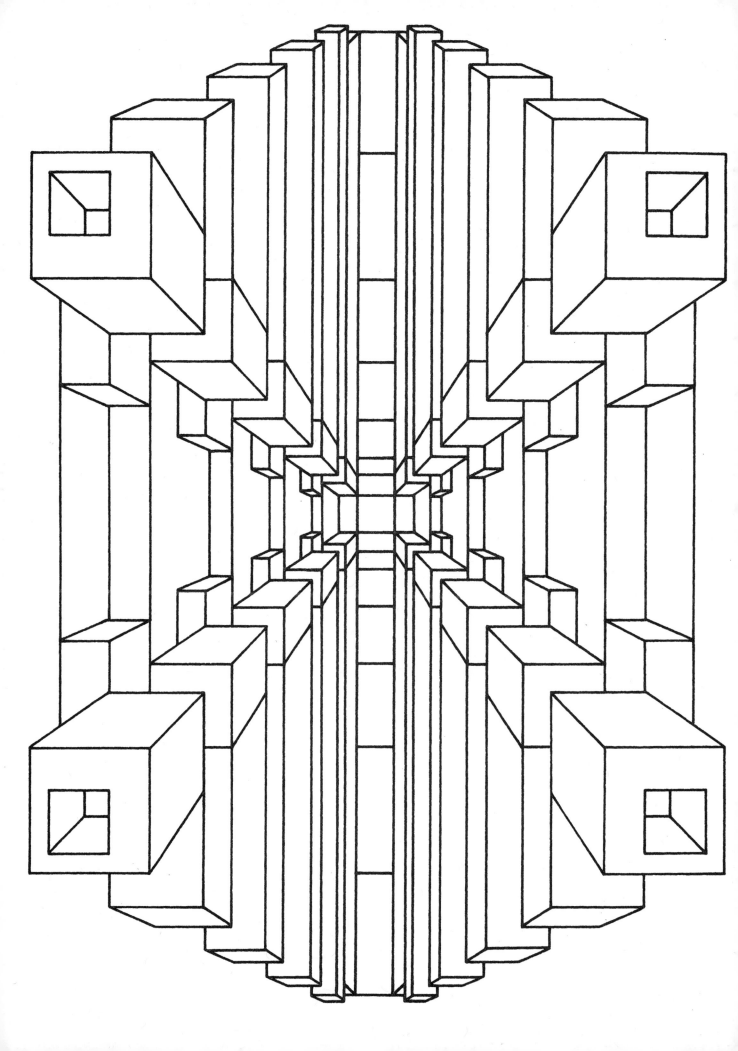

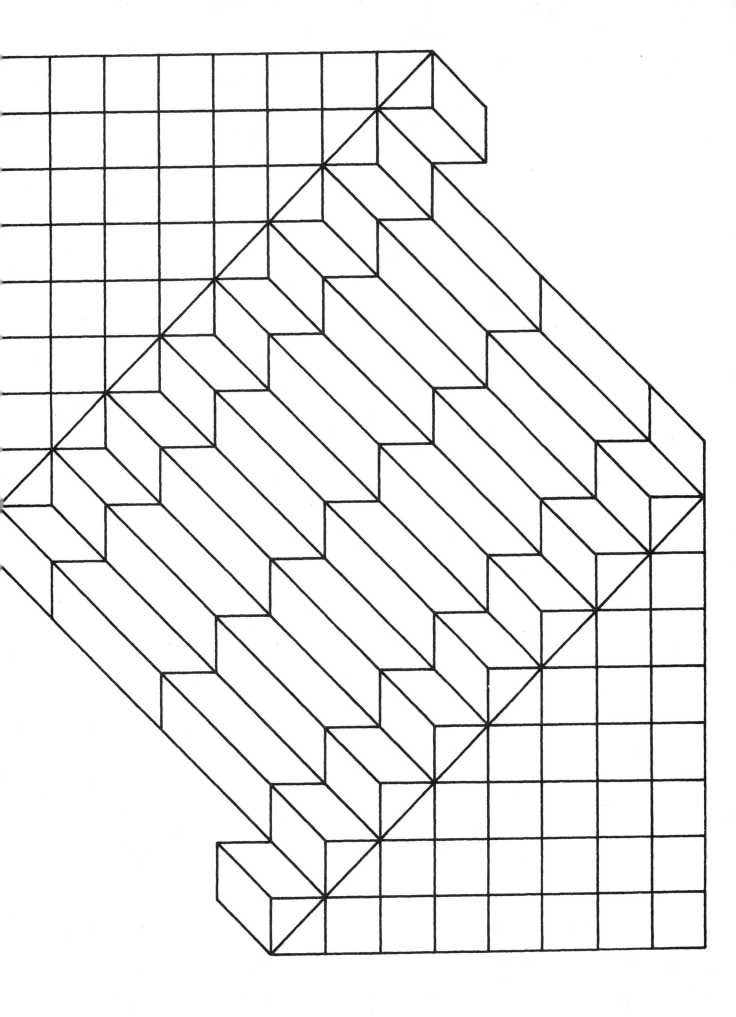

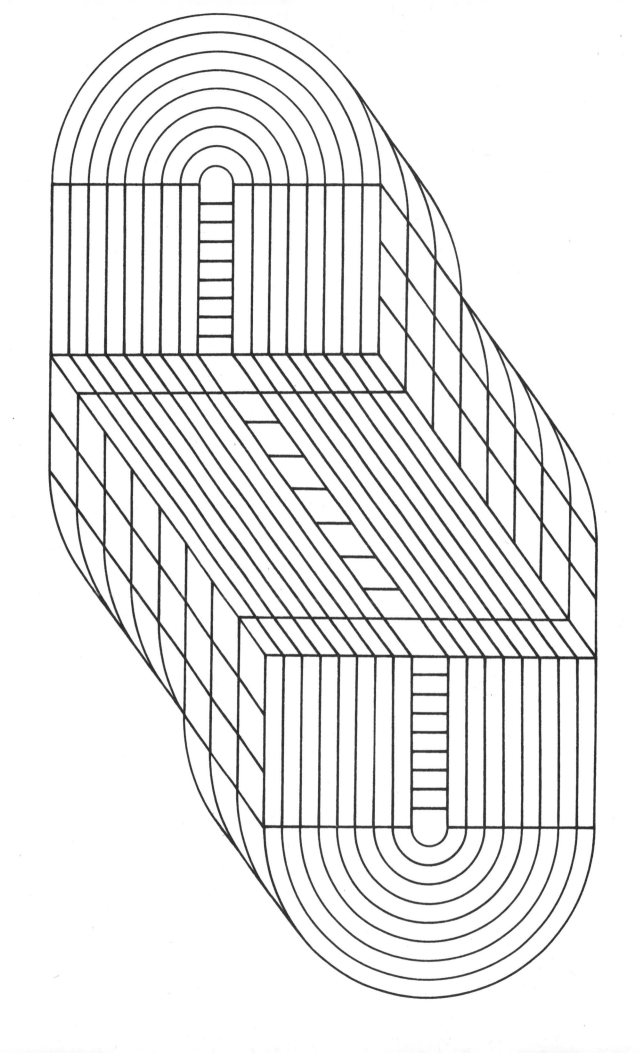

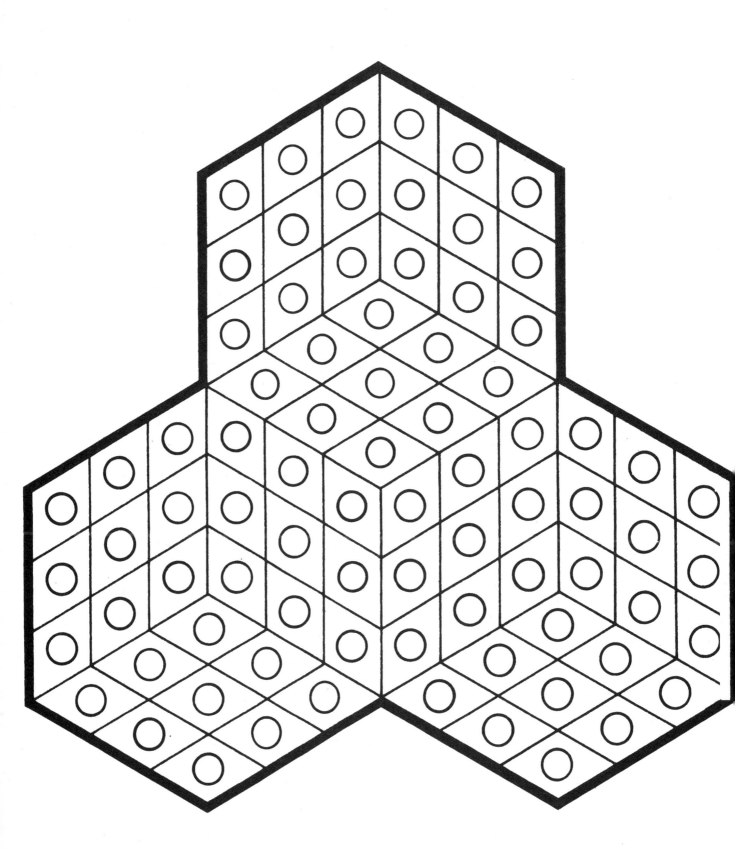

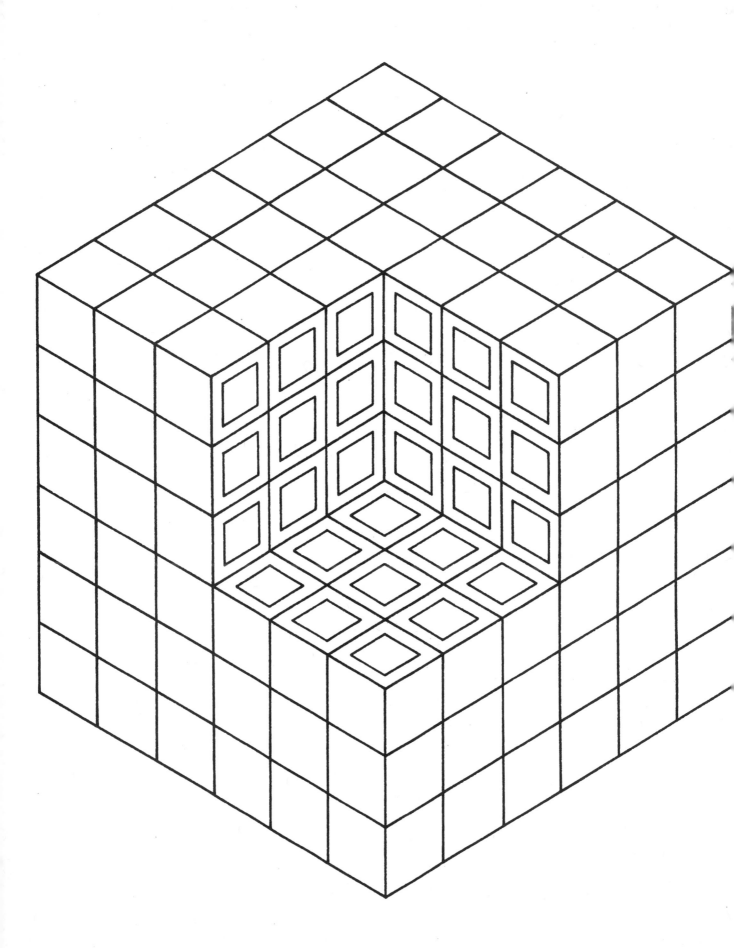

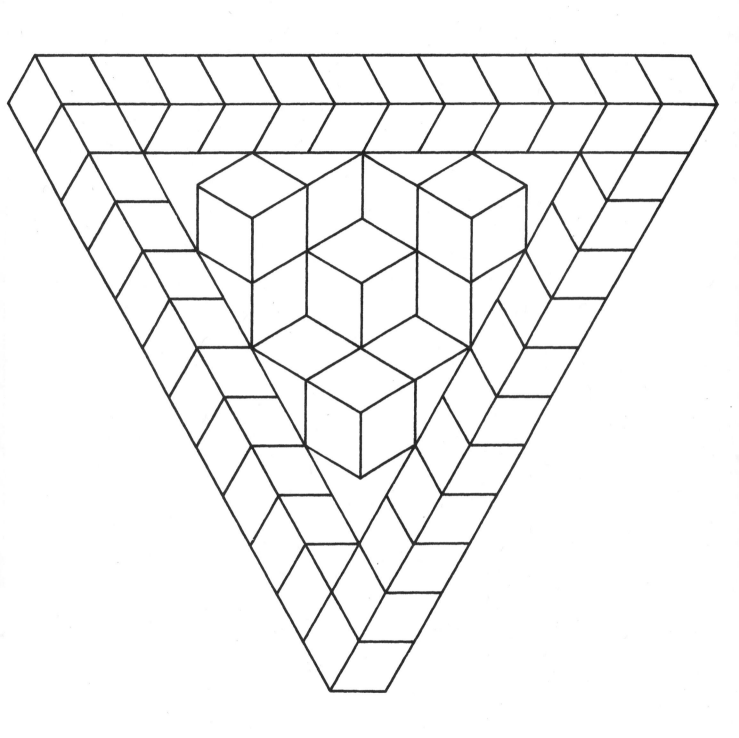

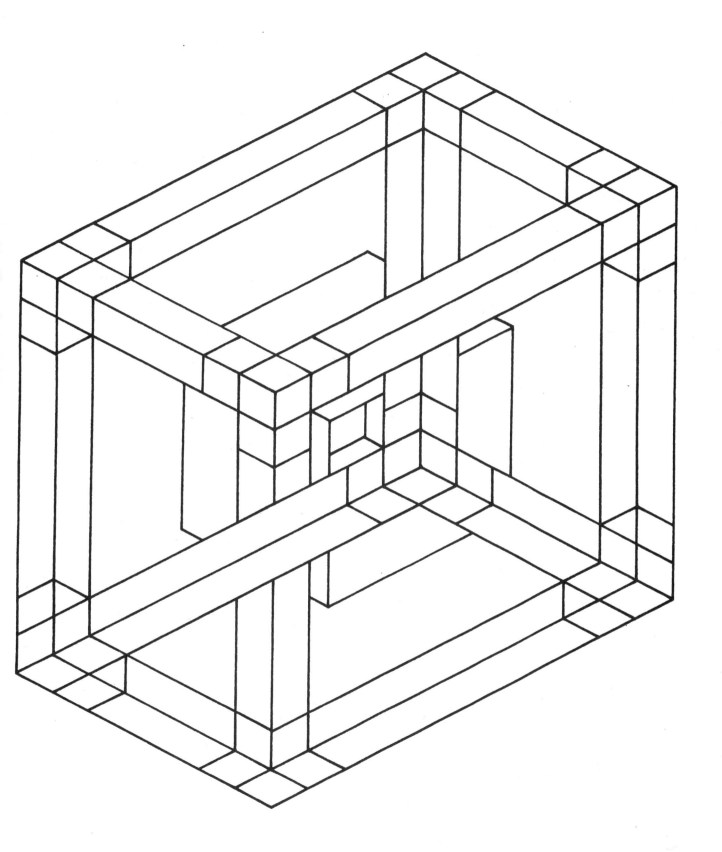

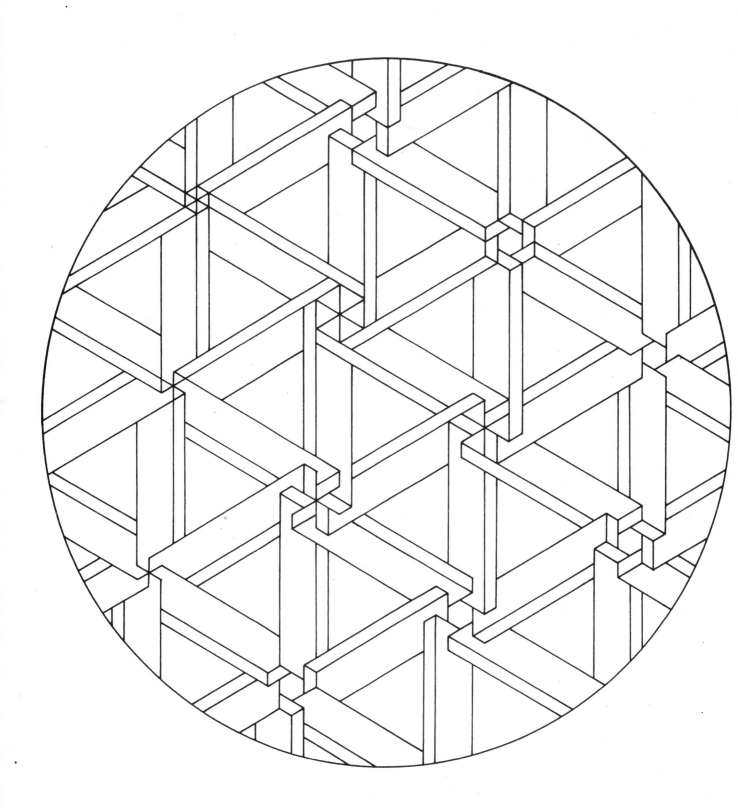

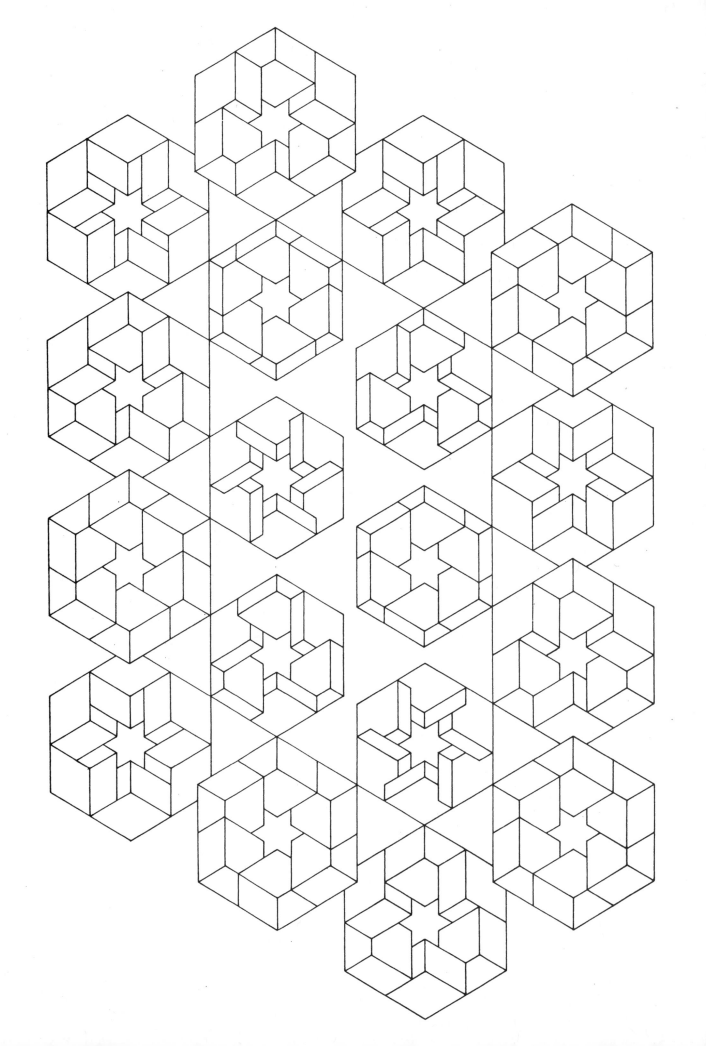

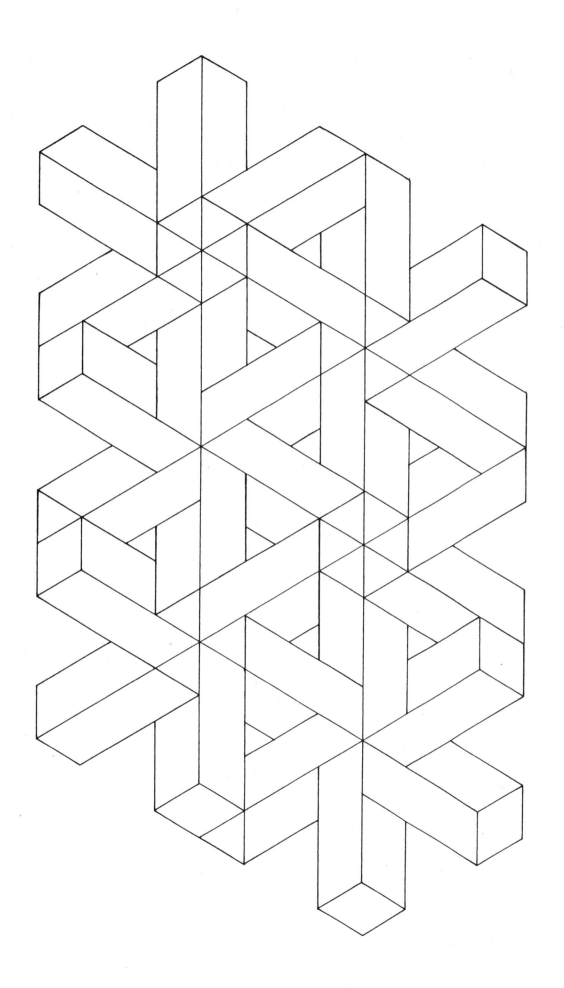

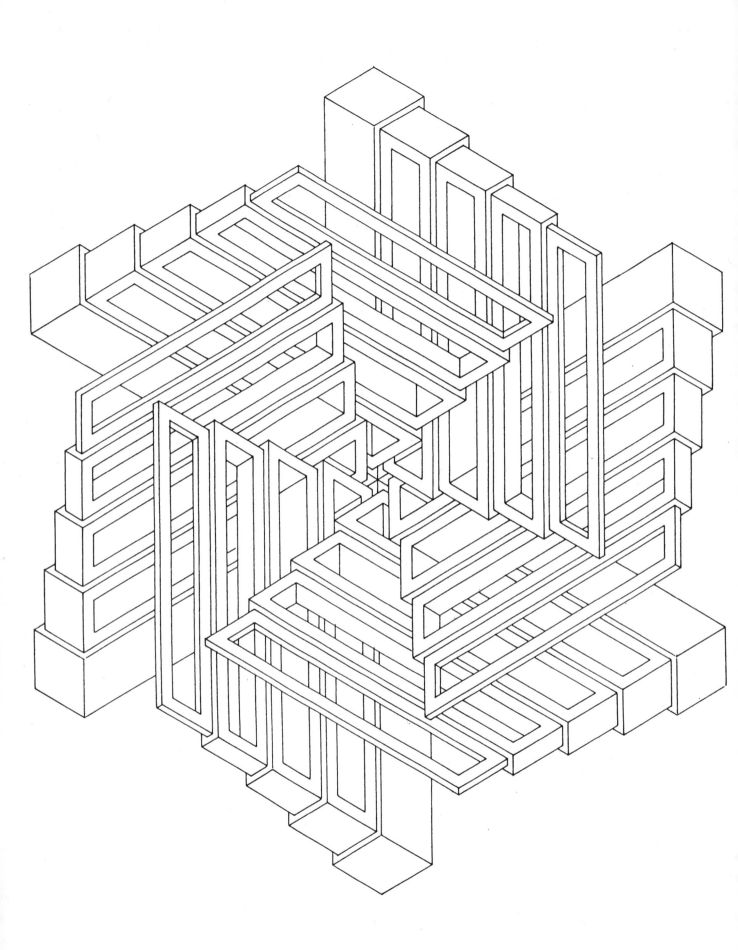

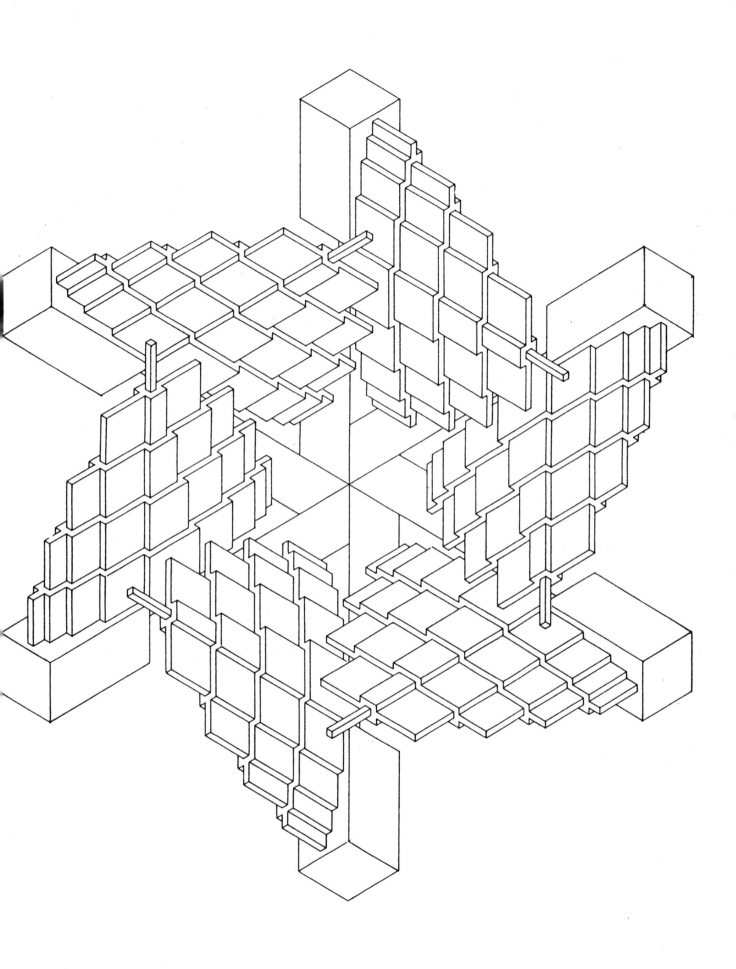

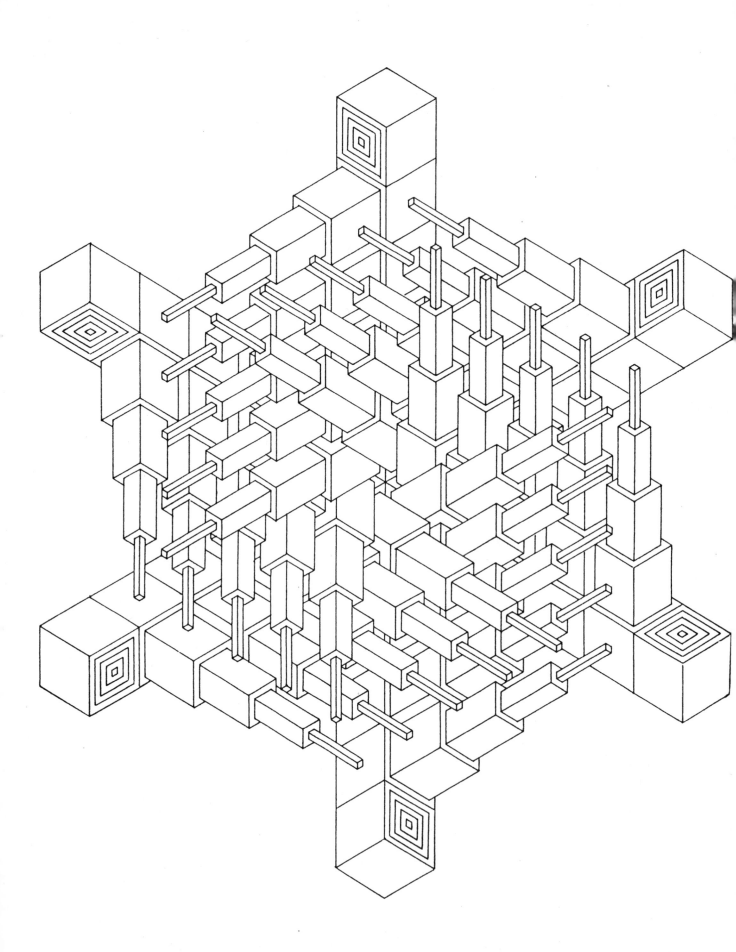

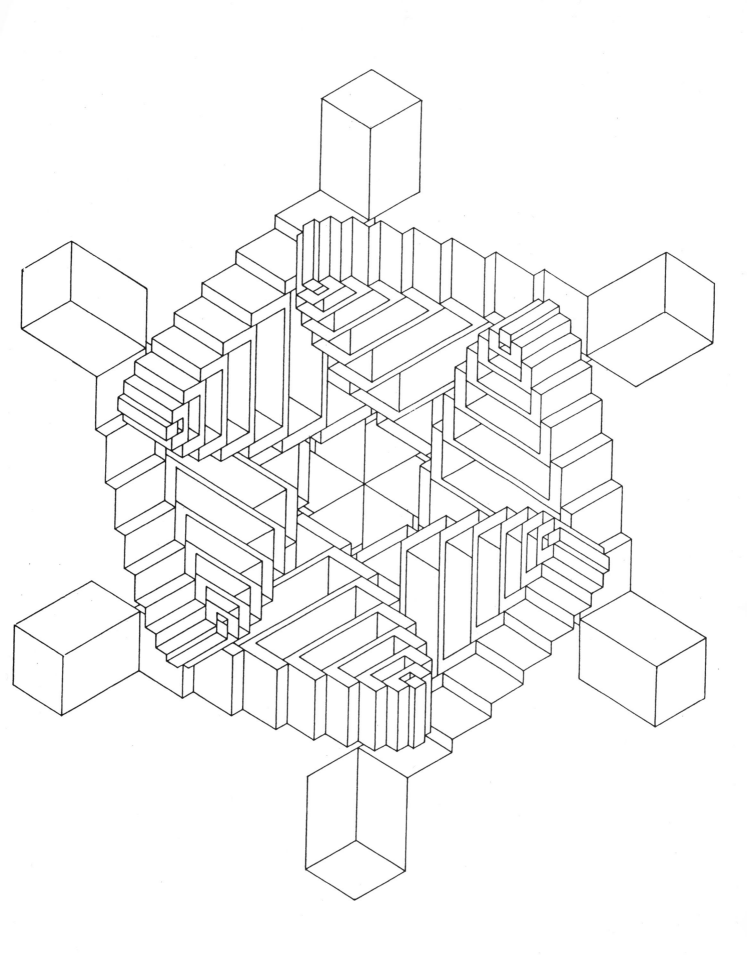

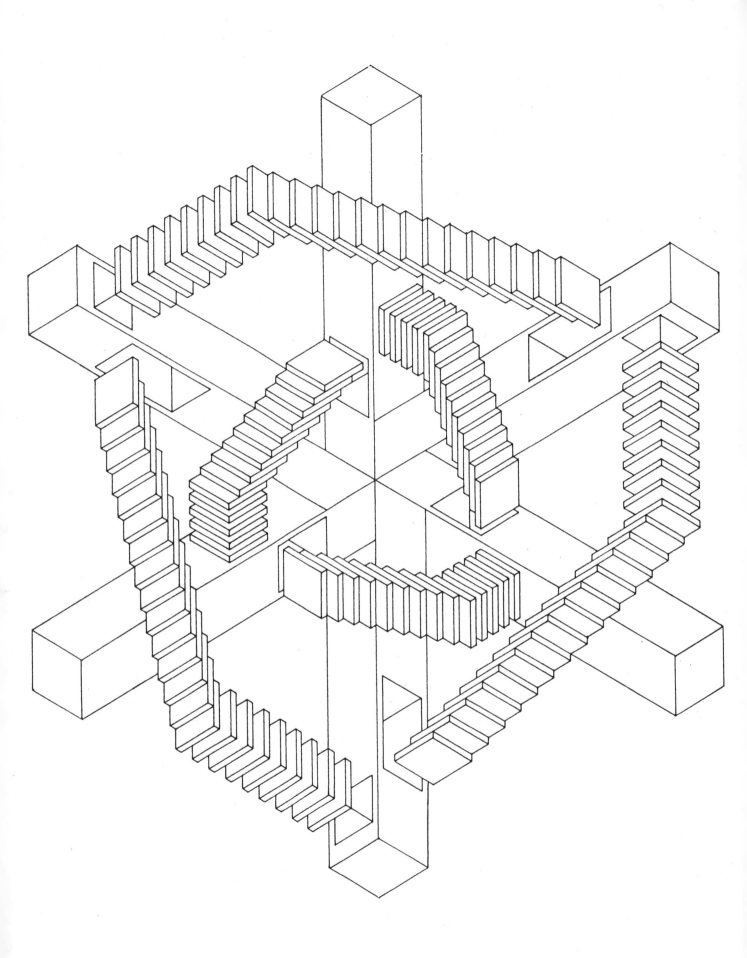

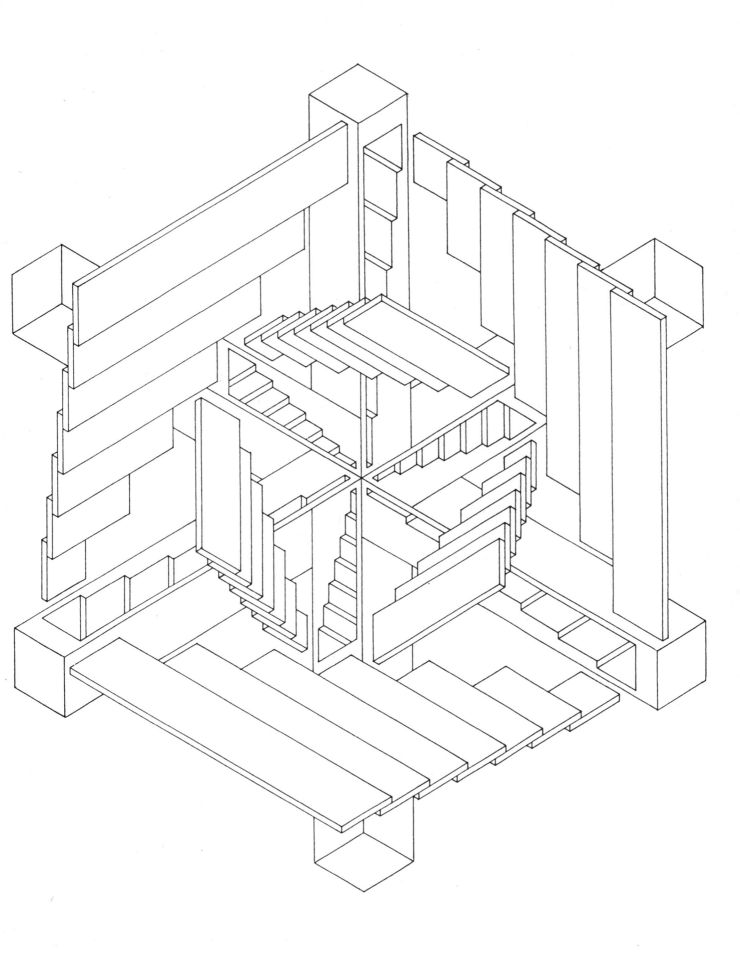

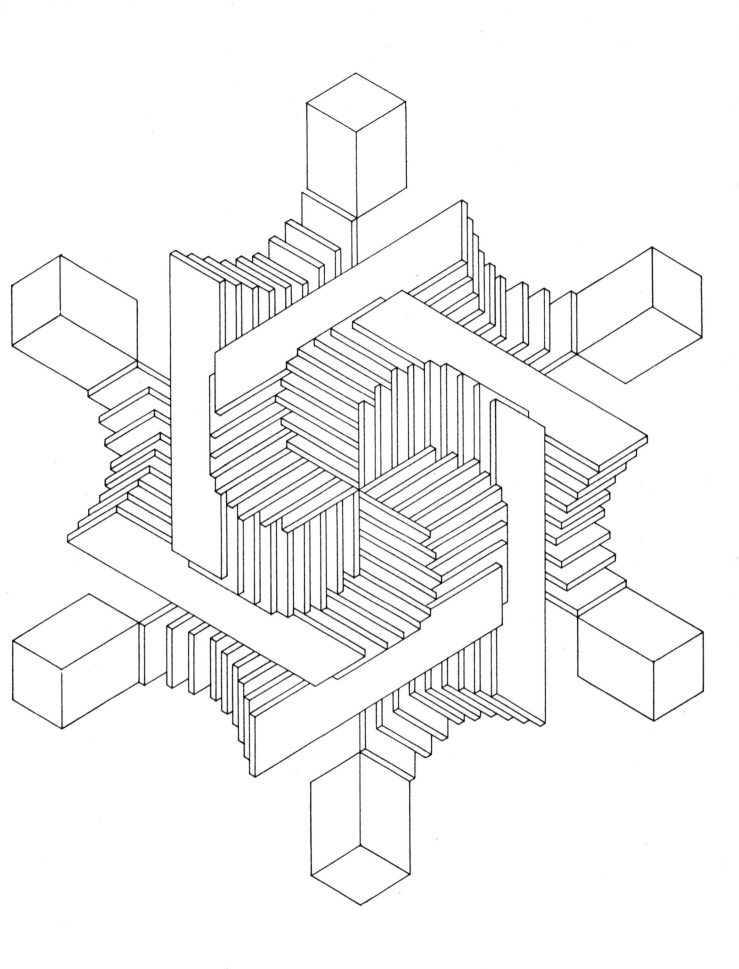

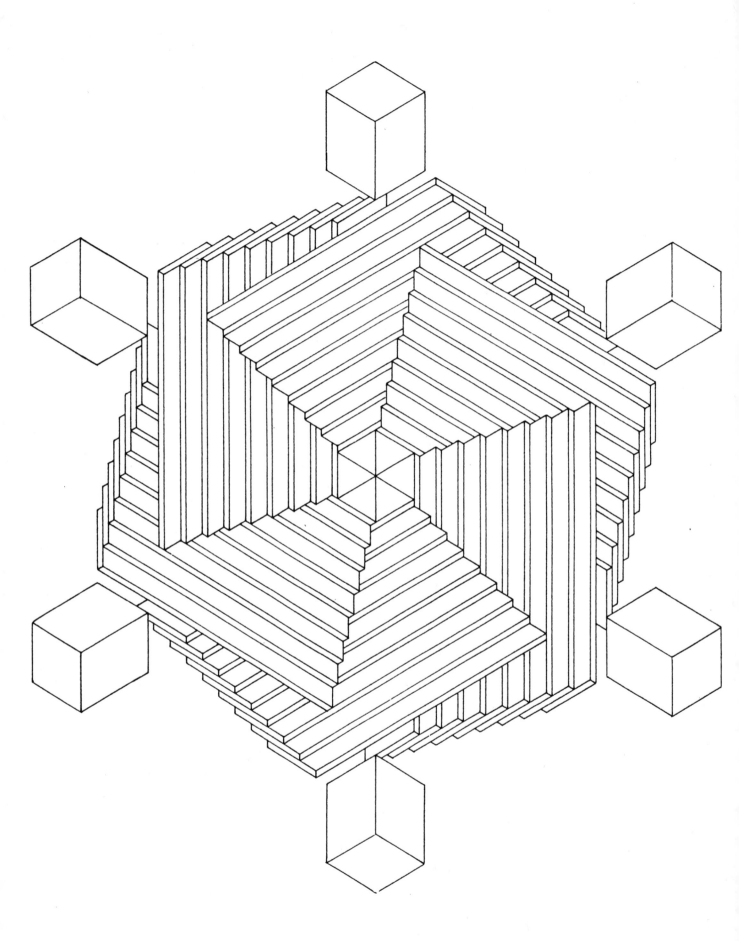

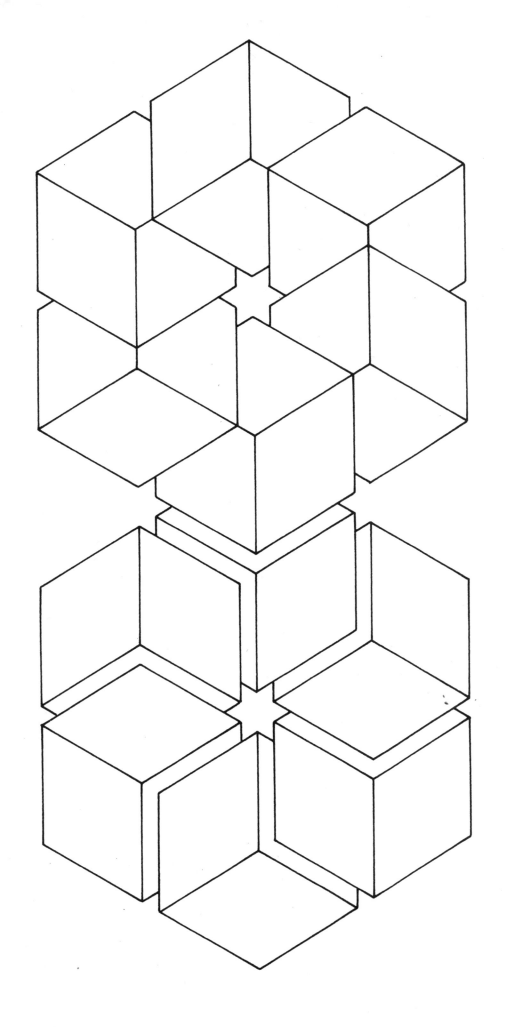